TAMING
YOUR
TO-DO
LIST

TAMING YOUR YOUR TO-DO LIST

glynnis whitwer

SPIRE

© 2015 by Glynnis Whitwer

Published by Revell
a division of Baker Publishing Group
PO Box 6287, Grand Rapids, MI 49516-6287
www.revellbooks.com

Spire edition published 2019
ISBN 978-0-8007-3602-6

Previously published in 2015 under the title *Taming the To-Do List*

Printed in the United States of America

All rights reserved. No part of this publication may be reproduced, stored in a retrieval system, or transmitted in any form or by any means—for example, electronic, photocopy, recording—without the prior written permission of the publisher. The only exception is brief quotations in printed reviews.

Unless otherwise indicated, Scripture quotations are from the Holy Bible, New International Version®. NIV®. Copyright © 1973, 1978, 1984, 2011 by Biblica, Inc.™ Used by permission of Zondervan. All rights reserved worldwide. www.zondervan.com. The "NIV" and "New International Version" are trademarks registered in the United States Patent and Trademark Office by Biblica, Inc.™

Scripture quotations labeled AMP are from the Amplified® Bible, copyright © 1954, 1958, 1962, 1964, 1965, 1987 by The Lockman Foundation. Used by permission.

Scripture quotations labeled ESV are from The Holy Bible, English Standard Version® (ESV®), copyright © 2001 by Crossway, a publishing ministry of Good News Publishers. Used by permission. All rights reserved. ESV Text Edition: 2007

Scripture quotations labeled NASB are from the New American Standard Bible®, copyright © 1960, 1962, 1963, 1968, 1971, 1972, 1973, 1975, 1977, 1995 by The Lockman Foundation. Used by permission.

Scripture quotations labeled NLT are from the *Holy Bible*, New Living Translation, copyright © 1996, 2004, 2007 by Tyndale House Foundation. Used by permission of Tyndale House Publishers, Inc., Carol Stream, Illinois 60188. All rights reserved.

Scripture quotations labeled NRSV are from the New Revised Standard Version of the Bible, copyright © 1989, by the Division of Christian Education of the National Council of the Churches of Christ in the United States of America. Used by permission. All rights reserved.

Published in association with the literary agency of Fedd & Company, Inc., PO Box 341973, Austin, TX 78734

19 20 21 22 23 24 25   7 6 5 4 3 2 1

To Tod, my husband and best friend.
Thank you for always believing in me,
and always supporting God's call on my life.
I love you.

Contents

Acknowledgments

I'm so grateful to God for letting me have so much fun serving Him and for putting me in such a loving family. Thanks to my husband, Tod, and my five blessings, Joshua, Dylan, Cathrine, Robbie, and Ruth, for supporting me while I wrote this book and let other things slide (but didn't procrastinate—read chapter 15).

I'm grateful for . . .

My mother, Kathryn, my sisters, Paula and Liz, and their families. I still think it's amazing we never have conflict at family gatherings.

My wonderful friends at Proverbs 31 Ministries. For Lysa Ter-Keurst and her godly leadership. For my executive team friends who didn't get frustrated with me for being late on a few things while writing this book. And for the staff, speakers, and writers at Proverbs 31 Ministries, who model God's grace and kindness. A special shout out to my "Word" team, who picked up the slack and prayed me through the finishing of this book: Barb, Steph, and Kenisha.

My friend Karen Ehman, who helps me see perspective when ministry and work get crazy.

Esther Fedorkevich, my agent, who took a chance on me. Thank you for sharing in my vision and believing in me.

Andrea Doering and the team at Revell. I'm so glad God answered the prayer of my heart from years ago to one day work with you.

The biggest thanks of all go to Jesus, my Savior, for giving me purpose and value that transcend my to-do list.

Introduction

Looking back, it's obvious procrastination has been a lifelong companion of mine.

It's always been easy to find other things to blame. But digging down deep unearths the truth—I put things off that I really should do. And in doing so, my to-do list gets out of control.

My procrastination first showed up in school, when I'd wait until the last minute to finish an assignment. Just good enough to make the grade . . . but never feeling like I'd done my best.

It then showed up at my first job, when I faced hard, challenging work that quite honestly made me wonder what I'd learned in four years of college. It was easier to plead busyness than to admit I felt underqualified and afraid to try. Would my work show I didn't have what it took?

Procrastination then popped up its bossy head as I got involved in church, volunteering, and leading small groups and Bible studies. But its influence truly escalated when I answered God's call to write and speak. It hasn't controlled all areas of my life, but it's impacted me enough that I finally said no. No to the lies that tomorrow would be easier. No to the fear that I'd look like a fool. No to the threat that my best wasn't good enough.

And I also finally said yes. Yes to addressing the underlying issues of my procrastination. Yes to being brave enough to face some weak areas. Yes to hard choices that bring my responsibilities under control. And yes to sharing it all with you.

Here's what you won't find in this book: advice written from someone who has only studied this topic in a classroom or laboratory. Or advice from someone standing on the sidelines with a megaphone yelling instructions. You won't find any advice like "Just do something" or "Get over yourself!"

Rather, what I hope and pray you'll find is encouragement from someone who knows all the doubts, frustration, and personal disappointment procrastination causes because she has lived it. But you'll also find hope, encouragement, and truth that procrastination doesn't define you. Plus I've included practical tools that have helped me, and others, face the reasons we delay addressing our highest and best work.

We're on even ground, you and me. And we're both standing in the shadow of the cross of Jesus, where there's much-needed grace to be found.

Thank you for joining me here.

In His love,

Glynnis

1

Procrastinate? Me?

God has promised forgiveness to your repentance; but he has not promised tomorrow to your procrastination.

St. Augustine

Is it possible that I'm a procrastinator? When this idea worked its way into my mind, I scoffed. After all, I was one of the busiest people I knew. Between work, home, kids, church, and my husband, my days were full to overflowing. I was always doing something for someone. I might put things off, but it was only because there was so much on my plate. *Right?*

I preferred to think of myself as a highly productive person. Have you ever heard the old adage that if you want something done, give it to the busiest person you know? Yep. That would be me.

Routinely I'd hear from a friend, "How do you manage all you do?" I usually responded with a humble brag such as, "Oh, I guess I'm just wired that way."

And my heart would do a little pitter-patter at this recognition of my work, at their respect of my achievements. I hungered for that type of response, and it fueled me to keep pressing on.

But in the quiet of my day, my to-do list whispered another truth. I knew this truth but I preferred to avoid it. It was easier to find excuses and place blame—because, after all, I was really busy.

You see, there's another side my friends don't see. They have the advantage of seeing all I get done; they don't see what's left undone.

But *I* do.

And it gnaws at my conscience. All. The. Time.

Perhaps you know this feeling too. No matter how much you do, what bothers you most is what you didn't do. That long list of to-dos (whether written down or just rolling around in your mind) keeps you up at night. It motivates you to download more productivity apps. You read every article on time management you can find.

And still you struggle to get things done. To manage all you have to do. And your list keeps growing. A lot of these tasks are mundane, everyday tasks. Things like cleaning the shower, making a menu for the week, and paying bills.

But there's more than just the required and necessary undone tasks that bother you. There are the dreams you cannot touch. The vacations you don't plan. The time you know you should spend with your parents, your children, your friends.

The "shoulds" of life trail us, tapping on our shoulders, saying, *Don't forget about me.*

Really? How could we? Those things we know we *should* do are never far away. It's hard to relax. Even when we try to take a break and enjoy some downtime, our minds don't stop. And then guilt sneaks in and joins the pressure party. It's an exhausting way to live. I know.

A few years ago I thought I was having a panic attack. I sat on my couch feeling as if I had a heavy weight on my chest. It was hard to breathe and anxiety simmered, but there was no apparent threat. However, there were looming deadlines, a demanding home business, part time telecommuting work, mounting emails, and five kids wondering when dinner would be ready and if there were any clean socks.

The problem wasn't what I was doing. It was everything I couldn't get done.

The Surface Problem

My life felt out of control. I was burned out from having too much to do and always feeling behind. The fear of disappointing someone chased me constantly. I was busy, but didn't know what else to do.

Turns out I didn't have an anxiety problem. I had an overcommitment problem.

After that day, I became like a detective. Was I really losing it, or had something else happened? I used to be able to manage my life; what had changed?

My personal study led me to some significant findings that helped me address a part of my problem. Life was changing around me, but I kept trying to manage the new world with old tools. And with today's fast pace, "old" can be just a few years.

The biggest change in society I identified was a shift in responsibility. The burden of communication had shifted from the sender to the receiver. You see, when I grew up, we didn't have email, or even answering machines. So the burden to get a message to me was on you. Now, people can reach me any time, any place. And the burden is on me to respond.

This shift has affected all of us. Here's what happened for me: rather than being proactive about my life I spent my days being reactive. Rather than being the manager of my life I was the minion, at the beck and call of others.

Not only was I shortchanging myself and my family with that approach but I also wasn't honoring and obeying God fully.

It took me time to understand what was happening and implement changes, but these changes made a huge difference in my life. Reordering my priorities and learning new ways to manage my workload brought a sense of peace I hadn't felt in years. This is definitely still an ongoing battle, but there is hope. As we go through this book, I'll share some of my choices with you.

But even though I made many smart changes in my life, I discovered my overcommitment issue had another layer underneath. There was another beast to face head-on. Its name was *procrastination*.

The Deeper Problem

Procrastination has always been a silent companion of mine, one that I knew was there but, as I said earlier, I preferred to ignore. My husband and I used to laugh and say if it wasn't for the last minute, nothing would get done. I didn't really think it was a problem. *Everyone procrastinates on something*, I reasoned. *Plus, what more can I do?* The problem certainly wasn't with me.

On the surface, there were always reasons why I couldn't get everything done. Good, solid reasons. It was just that I'd taken on too much work. Or my family's needs were too demanding. And the technology that should have made my life easier actually made it harder sometimes. Who couldn't understand that?

Then, faced with a deadline, I would stress out, snap at everyone, stay up late, and rush to finish what needed to be done. Consequently, everything suffered. My family paid the price, my work was subpar, and I became a person I didn't like very much.

The issues affecting me were all legitimate. But there was *still* another issue afoot. One that took some soul-searching to identify. It was an internal desire for ease rather than challenge.

Could It Go Deeper?

You see, faced with a choice between two tasks, my tendency was to choose whichever seemed easier at the moment. I desired an immediate benefit over a future blessing.

This truth about myself hit hard when I read Proverbs 13:4: "The appetite of the lazy craves, and gets nothing, while the appetite of the diligent is richly supplied" (NRSV).

I was actually using the verse to write a devotion about the importance of hard work when God made me sit for a while on the first half of it. I wasn't very happy with God's hint that I might need to consider laziness an issue. But the reality was my procrastination often indicated a hunger for something.

Sometimes it was comfort, such as when I chose to do something I knew how to do rather than pushing myself to learn something new. Other times it was safety, such as when I preferred to not deal with a hard or scary possibility. Or maybe I was hungering for the applause of others when they saw how much I got done.

There was a deeper issue brewing that needed my attention. But here's the bottom line, then and now: when my choices are fueled by self-focused need, my best work is seldom done.

The truth is, there's not much I won't put off until tomorrow in exchange for an easier task today. I'm always busy, so on the surface it looks like I'm accomplishing a lot. But I have to ask myself: *Is the work I do today my best work? Is it the most crucial work? Is it what will make the most positive and lasting impact on my life? On my family's lives? On my career? On my ministry?*

Of course, there are always unpleasant tasks that are easy to procrastinate on. Organizing for taxes. Deep cleaning the house. Going to the doctor's office. Those I put off as long as possible.

But I found I was also procrastinating on good things. On creative things. On dreams that would make my heart sing.

Some Reasons for My Procrastination

Here's an example of what I mean. As the director of communications at my work, I had an opportunity to create and teach classes. This was something I loved to do. It's my sweet spot. And I would make money doing it. Great reasons to jump in with both feet. Right?

But it also meant I would have to shift gears mentally in my day. I'd have to set aside other work to focus on this. I'd have to be creative. To research. To plan. To design.

I would also have to have a slide presentation, which meant I'd have to learn Keynote, and I always forgot how to make the bullets fly in and out. I couldn't remember what they called that function, so I couldn't even research it. The one slide presentation I did was with help, and I was so excited about how creative the flames burning up my title were, and I loved the sparkly bullet points. Then someone told me people didn't like fancy slideshows.

Great! Now I would have to learn how to prepare an effective slideshow. Without flames and sparkles.

Then once I had that done, I'd have to figure out the webinar software. And I KNEW there would be a technical glitch. The first time I tried by myself, there was no audio for the entire presentation. On my second attempt there was audio, but no video. Wonderful.

And for the record, just hitting random buttons on the keyboard doesn't help.

So back to that teaching opportunity. I knew I would get frustrated and impatient, and my emails would build up while I worked on it. Then someone would wonder why I hadn't responded to their email and send me another, albeit nice, follow-up email to crowd my in-box.

Just thinking about what it would take to create a class made me not even want to start!

It's much easier to try to get rid of some emails. Or bake cookies. That won't stress me out and there's a sweet reward at the end.

Sometimes I procrastinated because I didn't know the details, and the fear of the unknown kept me from moving forward. This happened when I learned about major dental work needed by one of my children.

The dentist asked me into her office, while holding a set of X-rays. My son reclined in the chair, a plastic bib covering his chest and an apologetic grin on his face. The dentist flipped a switch on the wall, put the X-rays up to a light box, and pointed out the crowded conditions in my son's mouth.

"Mrs. Whitwer, your son needs to have his wisdom teeth removed or he's going to have problems later."

"I understand," I replied, not really seeing what she saw but unwilling to question her professional opinion. I folded the referral, tucked it into my purse, and left with the intent to make calls the next day to get an estimate of the cost, find out our insurance coverage, and set an appointment.

But I didn't.

Truthfully, I was a bit annoyed and thought the dentist was slightly overreacting. I didn't get my wisdom teeth pulled as a child. Even though she referred us to a specialist, my suspicious nature was on alert. *Would she get a referral fee?*

I also dreaded the cost. Our finances were tight, and even with dental insurance the co-pay would certainly be more than we could afford. I didn't even want to know.

In the next year, two more dentists held two more sets of X-rays and told me the same diagnosis for two more children. The dentist explained the crowded conditions in one mouth and the wrong angle in the other.

By the time they handed me the third referral to a specialist, I was ready to get some pliers, watch a YouTube video, and take care of those teeth myself.

Maybe some mothers would have rushed right out and called the specialist after the first recommendation.

Some mothers might have put off the call for a few days. Some for a few weeks. Maybe some would even have delayed a few months.

Call me an overachiever, but I'm going on several years at this point.

· · · ·

So, where does this leave me? Ready to deal with this issue of procrastination once and for all. To uncover the reasons beneath my tendency to put off hard things. To discover why I delay progress on the highest and best callings on my life.

Without addressing the issue of procrastination, my days can be filled with busywork but not my best work.

Busywork is the thief of our best work. It's answering emails rather than starting to write that novel. It's replying to texts rather than filling out the adoption paperwork. It's arranging meetings rather than drawing up the plans for an innovative project at work.

It's not always the big projects we delay. Sometimes my best work is caring for my home and family. I can go on Pinterest for menu ideas, but the fashion pins are so cute and forty-five minutes later I still don't have a plan for dinner. There's always something easier to do than clean the house, fold laundry, make doctor's appointments, organize paper piles, and so on.

We have things upside down! The things that matter least replace the things that matter most in our schedules. The work that would make the greatest impact on our lives gets put at the bottom of our to-do lists and transferred from one list to another—so many times they eventually fall off.

Sometimes it's near impossible to figure out what is our best work. It sounds so easy to say, "Identify your priorities and do those first." However, when we have so many demands on our time, requests for our attention, and needs we must meet, we can feel helpless. We can feel like we don't know what to do next.

Feelings of helplessness make us want to escape, avoid, numb. It's right here where we make the choice to put off the very thing that would make the most impact.

When those feelings start to overtake me, it's time for me to press pause rather than make a self-defeating choice. Sometimes, the best thing to do is nothing . . . except seek direction from the One who always knows what our best is.

It's hard to differentiate between good, better, and best. There are so many options, choices, and demands. If left to my own instincts, when I'm feeling overwhelmed I can run in circles. Much like going to the grocery store, spending a hundred dollars, and leaving with nothing for dinner.

This is when we desperately need wisdom beyond what we can muster to make the best choices for ourselves, our families, our ministries, and our companies. Knowledge gives us facts, but wisdom gives us truth that makes a difference.

To find wisdom, I need to silence the demands of many to hear the commands of One. God is faithful, and His Word promises we can receive wisdom. In fact, it's a gift from God. Here is what James 1:5–6 says:

> If any of you lacks wisdom, you should ask God, who gives generously to all without finding fault, and it will be given to you. But when you ask, you must believe and not doubt, because the one who doubts is like a wave of the sea, blown and tossed by the wind.

Verse 6 holds the key to receiving wisdom: don't doubt. When we ask God for direction, we must trust that He will speak to us. When I second-guess God, I get into trouble. We'll explore this idea more in a later chapter, but for now, know there is help.

Procrastination is a dangerous habit to develop, and it carries a high cost not only to our schedules but also to our hearts, spiritual lives, relationships, and finances. There's a snowball effect of delayed tasks. And as they accumulate, we are further from the life we want and from the person we want to be. We even procrastinate when God gives us an assignment, and then we walk in disobedience. Which creates entirely new issues.

The Promise of Tomorrow?

The heart of a procrastinator believes tomorrow is a promise. However, when we are honest with ourselves, we know God hasn't promised that. We aren't guaranteed tomorrow. In fact, we aren't even promised the rest of this day. We are stewards of the only moment we are given—which is now.

When we procrastinate on the things we know we should do, we are assuming a confidence in the future that is unwise. In fact, the Bible even goes so far as to call it *sin*.

> Look here, you who say, "Today or tomorrow we are going to a certain town and will stay there a year. We will do business there and make a profit." How do you know what your life will be like tomorrow? Your life is like the morning fog—it's here a little while, then it's gone. What you ought to say is, "If the Lord wants us to, we will live and do this or that." Otherwise you are boasting about your own pretentious plans, and all such boasting is evil. Remember, it is sin to know what you ought to do and then not do it. (James 4:13–17 NLT)

These verses aren't saying "Don't make plans." They are advising us to submit our plans to the Lord and be obedient to Him and His timing.

There are times when God says *wait*. Sometimes we do get ahead of God and focus on our own plans. But in this book, I'm going to address the opposite problem—when God is saying *go* and we say no.

Verse 17 sends a clear message to procrastinators: "Remember, it is sin to know what you ought to do and then not do it" (NLT).

Thankfully, procrastination is also an issue we can address. When we are honest about ourselves, and make simple changes in how we think and act, we can immediately impact our lives. We can turn our days around, focusing our best energy on our highest priorities. And we can tame those multipage to-do lists.

My goal in dealing with procrastination isn't to get more done. I want to get more of the *right* things done. And eliminate the nagging guilt that keeps me from fully resting and enjoying downtime.

Our best work pushes us, challenges us, and stretches us. It's what we were created to do, and it will demand our highest focus and attention. But the rewards will be just as great.

Is it time for you to deal with procrastination in your life too? Would you like to join me? I'm pretty sure we'll have more success together than if we try this alone.

PRACTICAL APPLICATION

I imagine you have thoughts about what you'd like to change in your life. Perhaps you have some everyday tasks that pile up, like laundry or mail. Or you have some goals that seem too big so you ignore them, like planning a vacation or organizing your craft room.

Rather than feel overwhelmed, what if you identified two tasks or projects you'd like to tackle? Just two. One small and one large. Imagine what it would feel like to finally manage those areas well . . . to finally pursue that dream of your heart. How would it impact your daily life? Would you have more peace? Would you have more joy? More purpose?

If you'd like to end this book with at least two areas of success, I invite you to identify those two areas right now. Write them on this page or in a journal. We'll revisit your progress as we move through the book. I believe God will give you personal insight into the reasons behind your procrastination, and together we'll find practical ways to get you started.

I'd like to better manage this regular task:

I'd like to address this personal goal:

2

What Is Procrastination?

Everybody delays doing something, but not every delay is procrastination. There are good reasons why we put off certain tasks. Sometimes we don't have the supplies or the information we need. Other times we don't have the money. Most of the time, the honest reasons for delay are due to a shifting of priorities.

With small priorities, this is an ongoing process. A friend has a flat tire and is stranded at the mall, so you put down your project and head to her rescue. Or changes in priority can be big, like when our family adopted two girls from Africa and discovered their needs went beyond what we had anticipated. That act of obedience caused me to stop pursuing dreams I'd had for years as I set aside one set of goals and replaced them with another.

Life is full of surprises. Those that make us smile with delight, the everyday variety that feel mundane, and those that bring us to our knees.

A wise woman knows when it's time to put the brakes on a project and turn to the needs God has placed in front of her. The Bible tells many stories of people whose lives were redirected. One example in the New Testament is the story Jesus told about the good Samaritan who took a detour to tend to a wounded man. Caring for a beaten and bruised stranger was certainly not on the Samaritan's agenda. Jesus used this story to show us the importance of putting the needs of our neighbors above our own at times.

Blessed are those who listen and watch for what new thing God is about.

Procrastination, however, is a completely different issue.

We might blame the surprise need as the cause of our delay, but true procrastination involves a voluntary delay of something we could do but choose not to. Although it might include a shifting of priorities, its root cause is our resistance toward the task.

In other words, procrastination is an intentional delay of something that is in our best interest to do. For instance, it is in my best interest to exercise. And I could do it. I have an affordable gym membership. I can make time in my day. But the truth is, I don't like exercise. There's not even a sport I like to play.

Some people talk about feeling great once they start working out. In fact, studies show exercise releases feel-good endorphins in a person's brain and should provide that so-called runner's high. I think my endorphins run and hide when I start to work out, because all I feel is sweaty. And like I need a Diet Coke. But it would raise some eyebrows if I brought my bottle of soda to the gym. So, given the slightest reason to change my plans, I do. *Tomorrow I will feel more like exercising.* Right?

If a friend calls with a flat tire as I am about to go to the gym, I secretly celebrate a reason to put off going to the gym. Of course, once I'm done helping, I rationalize that it's too late to fit a workout in and cancel my plans, certain I'll go the next day. But on most days it probably is still possible for me to go to the gym.

I've also been going to lose my "baby weight" . . . for about nineteen years. Which just so happens to be the age of my youngest son. Every day I wake up with the best intentions to start my new healthy eating plan, and that lasts until I actually have to deny myself something I enjoy.

A common excuse for me is when one of my college-age children calls and asks if I'm free for lunch. Of course I am! But rather than choose a salad, I celebrate our glorious time together and pick pizza. I could make a healthier choice but I don't.

Maybe you've got similar frustrations. Are there things you know you should do . . . you have the ability to do . . . truth be told, you have the time and resources to do . . . but you simply don't do?

Me too.

We all procrastinate to some extent. We all make choices to delay doing the things that would make a positive impact on our lives. And there's not much we won't delay. We put off everyday tasks like cleaning, filing papers, ironing, and home maintenance. We put off important things like doctor's appointments, paying bills, and making meal plans.

We put off spiritually enriching practices like praying, reading our Bibles, or serving others. We put off relationship-building choices like forgiveness, addressing an offense from a friend, or even spending time with people who are important to us.

And we put off our own dreams, things like going back to school, changing careers, adopting children, or taking a vacation. Sadly, most of us don't even get to the dream stage because we know what will happen. We know that we'll get excited, make plans, maybe even get started—and then things will fizzle. And perhaps we don't even understand why.

For some, this pattern happens again and again, bringing feelings of frustration, disappointment, and discouragement. Perhaps you've even labeled yourself a failure, certain you'll never finish anything. Oh, how I understand.

Most of us have gone through a similar cycle and felt similar feelings. We've felt the despair. We've felt the condemnation. Perhaps just knowing you aren't alone will help. Procrastination has a common cycle; see if you can identify yourself in it.

The Procrastination Cycle

In their book *Procrastination*, authors Jane B. Burka, PhD, and Lenora M. Yuen, PhD, identify a six-stage cycle of procrastination that is common to most.[1] This cycle can happen in hours, days, weeks, or months. The timing can vary, but the thoughts and emotions we share are similar.

Stage One: I'll Start Early This Time

The moment you make a decision to do something, you declare that this time you won't procrastinate. You *won't* wait until the last minute. You may not start right then, but you are confident you won't delay.

Stage Two: I've Got to Start Soon

At this stage, the early start is no longer possible. But it's still not the last minute. Anxiety starts to creep in each time you think about what you need to do.

Stage Three: What If I Don't Start?

All optimism is gone now. You realize you are on the cycle again and regret steps in. Burka and Yuen have me pegged perfectly when they say, "It is extremely common for procrastinators at this stage to do anything and everything except the avoided project."[2]

Isn't that the truth? Perhaps this is a good time to make a confession: I procrastinated on writing this book. Most authors will tell you their biggest challenge while writing a book will involve the topic of the book. My friend Lysa TerKeurst, when writing her book *The Best Yes* (which is on making wise decisions), says she couldn't make even the smallest decisions about it.

I should have seen it coming when I decided to write a book on procrastination. But that optimism of stage one was strong.

After getting the contract, I intended to start right away. But it was summertime and my kids had more flexible schedules. Then I was organizing a large part of an annual conference. My three college-age sons and my sister moved the next month. Then I took my mom on a ten-day trip. One thing after another became convenient excuses, and I started later than I wanted to start. But interestingly, each time I'd sit down to start, something else that I'd put off would hit my mind—and up I'd jump to go tackle it. Anything but keep my rear in a chair and my fingers typing. Stage three in action!

Can you imagine the snickers when friends and family asked me how the book writing was coming along? Yeah, it was embarrassing.

If you're reading this now, you know I finally finished the book. But it wasn't without applying all the things I'm writing about.

Stage Four: There's Still Time

Although your heart and mind are filled with discouragement and you feel like a fraud, there's still a sliver of hope that you'll finish on time.

Stage Five: There's Something Wrong with Me

When excuses have evaporated and there's no one left to blame, you realize once again the problem lies with *you*. You might start comparing yourself to others, wondering what they have that you don't. You believe there is something fundamentally wrong with you. Maybe you are missing an important personality characteristic or talent that everyone else has.

Stage Six: The Final Choice: To Do or Not to Do

It's at this point you either abandon the project or nearly kill yourself and alienate others as you summon every last ounce of effort and slide into home plate, dust flying and scrapes on your leg, with milliseconds to spare.

Sadly, even if you finish you don't feel good about it, because you know it wasn't your best effort.

. . . .

Does this cycle sound familiar? Perhaps you feel helpless and hopeless to break it. Do you wonder if you'll ever be free from the guilt and shame that we procrastinators can feel?

Here's some good news: just acknowledging the problem and the cycle is the beginning of breaking it. We aren't forever chained to being women who procrastinate. We can make changes in our daily habits. But one of the problems with procrastination is it's not always a conscious decision.

Why would we put off things that would improve our lives? It makes no sense. But we do it.

It's Not Always Conscious

As I've tried to get to the root of my procrastination habit, I started with the same question: Why?

That should be an easy question to answer. Why *do* I procrastinate?

For most things in life, with just a little thought, I can discover the *why* behind my choices—good and bad. My motivation is clear. I understand why I dislike exercise (it hurts), why I tend to overeat (food tastes so good), and why I put off ironing (it's boring).

But procrastination doesn't always provide such easy motivators. Sometimes, there's no simple *why* because there's no clear-cut problem. We procrastinators can put off anything! Pleasant and unpleasant. Fun and boring. Simple and complicated.

I'm still surprised at the tasks and projects I can procrastinate on. I can delay addressing small tasks that would only take a few minutes, important tasks that help me accomplish goals, and loving tasks that would bring a smile to someone else. And many times I've delayed something so long that I just gave up.

I've already listed some common things people delay, but let me share some of my personal procrastination challenges. They might surprise you, because you would never put off what I do. But it will prove my point that getting to the root of procrastination can be complicated.

Here are some of the things I've put off:

- Planning a night out with friends
- Shopping for a new outfit
- Making a doctor's appointment
- Dusting
- Organizing photos (I may never get to these)
- Calling a drywall repairman to fix a hole in the ceiling from a leak
- Planning a vacation
- Tackling an important project at work
- Redecorating my bedroom
- Sending birthday cards

If you made a list like this for yourself, you'd probably start to see the same thing I see—there's no apparent logical, consistent reason why we procrastinate.

The results for each of the tasks on my list would be worth the effort. It might mean better relationships, improved health, more peace at home, more professional opportunities, and increased income.

So why do I put them off?

The answers are there. It will take digging and introspection. However, once we identify the reasons for our delay, we can deal with them. Or in other words, when we know the *why*, we can strategize the *how*. We'll dig deeper into this question in upcoming chapters, but for now let's look at some general reasons.

A Self-Regulation Challenge

Procrastination isn't a character trait that some of us are assigned. It isn't common to one personality type over another. Although some of us are more relational and some are more project oriented, we all have the ability to procrastinate. Producers may delay relational issues, and those driven by relationships may delay projects. And vice versa.

Whatever our natural bent, procrastination happens due to a self-regulation failure based on an aversion to a negative emotion. Basically, we know what we should do (or not do) but we make choices against what we know is best in order to avoid discomfort somewhere in the midst of the process.

Self-regulation is a critical development skill we acquire, starting in childhood, that underlies our behavior. It's the capacity to control our impulses. It stops us from screaming at our bosses even though we *want* to. It motivates us to wash the dishes even though we *don't want* to. It's what gives us the ability to make choices that are in our best interest and are consistent with our personal goals and priorities. Without a strong sense of self regulation, we will act in ways that can cause guilt, shame, and anxiety . . . much like what we experience with procrastination.

Research consistently shows that self-regulation is critical for long-term well-being. If it's such an important skill, why is it so hard to develop? Although there are solid psychological approaches to improving self-regulation, there is also a truth that helps me understand why I make choices that negatively impact my goals: I am a sinful being living in a sinful world.

A Sin Problem

This isn't a popular notion among secular professionals. It's more acceptable to say we are basically good. However, the Bible clearly states the opposite. If we were good, we wouldn't have any trouble doing the right thing. But we all face this challenge and we all do things we regret.

In fact, I'm not the first follower of Jesus to struggle with making right choices. In Romans 7, the apostle Paul shares his frustration:

> For I know that good itself does not dwell in me, that is, in my sinful nature. For I have the desire to do what is good, but I cannot carry it out. For I do not do the good I want to do, but the evil I do not want to do—this I keep on doing. Now if I do what I do not want to do, it is no longer I who do it, but it is sin living in me that does it. (vv. 18–20)

This verse is not saying procrastination is sin, although it might be, if God has told you to do something. Rather, Paul recognizes there is a conflict within us that is caused by sin.

Sin entered the world at the beginning of our human story; it was served on a fruit platter in the Garden of Eden. Since then, we have opened the door to an enemy who actively plots our downfall. Satan knows he will not beat God in the end, but his goal is to foil God's plan and destroy God's followers in the meantime.

Satan knows our sin and uses it against us. And what better way to limit the power of God's kingdom than by getting God's followers to not do what they know they should?

But lest I leave you in a state of despair, we have hope. We have been given a power greater than the enemy's power.

The apostle John speaks of this enemy and the evil spirits in the world when he says, "You, dear children, are from God and have overcome them, because the one who is in you is greater than the one who is in the world" (1 John 4:4).

As followers of God, we have been given the power of God living in us. But so many of us neglect this power when it comes to the everyday challenges of life. We think thoughts like, *I'll always be this way*, or *It's impossible to change*.

But here's a freeing truth I've learned and want to pass on to you. Plant it deep in your heart so those untrue statements can't find a place to grow roots and linger: procrastination isn't a sign of our abilities or a statement of our value or worth. It's not a disqualified stamp on our lives or a banner of failure. It's not a label that we are lazy or disorganized.

In fact, I love that the apostle Paul clearly states the problem isn't him: "Now if I do what I do not want to do, it is no longer I who do it, but *it is sin living in me that does it*" (Rom. 7:20, emphasis added).

Procrastination isn't a sign there's something wrong with us but that there's opportunity for growth in our lives. And that's good news! We all have potential that is untapped. We have skills and talents to develop. And we have work yet to do.

Ephesians 2:10 says, "For we are God's handiwork, created in Christ Jesus to do good works, which God prepared in advance for us to do."

God has a good plan and a purpose for us. And we can have the greatest intentions to fulfill that plan. However, if we procrastinate to the point of abandoning our best work, or if we rush at the last minute and produce only a shadow of our potential product, all our good intentions will not amount to much.

No matter our age or season of life, we can each tend to a little personal "housekeeping" and strengthen those areas of our lives we have neglected. Addressing procrastination is an opportunity for us to do some honest self-reflection about why we choose to do certain tasks over others. That's basically the problem of procrastination in a nutshell.

It's not that we don't get things done—we don't get the right things done. The God-ordained things. The things that will make the most positive impact on our lives or the lives of those we love. And sometimes we delay addressing the highest and best callings on our lives.

Those are the things that cause the greatest regrets.

So getting to the root of the problem, getting to the *why*, will take work. But I'm convinced that when we get to the *why* we will uncover powerful motivators that we can use to help us move in the right direction.

● PRACTICAL APPLICATION

The next step in unraveling the complicated problem of procrastination is to look at reasons why we put off doing what we should do. In this chapter I defined procrastination as "a voluntary delay of something we could do but choose not to." Consider the two items you listed at the end of chapter 1. Are these things you could do but choose not to? If so, consider the idea of self-regulation presented here and the idea of avoiding discomfort. What is the discomfort you are avoiding in each of these areas?

The discomfort I experience with my regular task is:

The discomfort in addressing my personal goal is:

3

Understanding
Some of the Whys

Few of us choose to put ourselves in hard places. In fact, we spend most of our lives trying to avoid them. We look for ways to do things easier, faster, and more efficiently. Shortcuts are coveted. And we look to eliminate the hard parts of most jobs by finding a trick or tip to help.

But what if all that search for ease does us a disservice?

What if rather than looking for the easy way out we should be pressing in to the hard places of life? Could it be that we're actually weakening our resolve to face life's challenges? Both those that are big and life-changing, and those that are small and everyday.

I've seen this in my life as I've uncovered my underlying desire for comfort, which affects my ability to achieve my goals. This truth about my comfort-seeking self was first revealed to me a few years ago, when I got overly ambitious and signed up for a cardio training class at a mixed martial arts gym. My three teenage sons and husband were taking classes there, and a part of me wanted their affirmation. I wanted to prove to them and myself that I could do it too. And since, as you now know, I have an aversion to exercise, I hoped to be motivated by them.

So I bought some new tennis shoes and some comfortable trendy workout clothes and started with enthusiasm. However, it was quickly apparent that my expectations of myself were too high. I began to think I should have started with something more my speed—like walking to the mailbox.

A month into my exercise program I wanted to quit. On days when we had class I woke up absolutely dreading it. And since the class started at 5:00 p.m., these were very long days.

With the encouragement of my family, I pressed on and ignored my body's protests. But each week I discovered a new pain somewhere in my body; my shins, knees, and arms all groaned with the discomfort of being woken so roughly from their sedentary state.

During one grueling exercise class a few months in, the instructor had us do a lower back exercise. At the first twinge of pain, I stopped. I knew that some pain could be dangerous, and I didn't want to continue something that could do damage to my back. The instructor noticed, and stooped down to my level with a questioning look on his face. "It hurts," I whispered, not wanting to draw attention to my weakness.

"I know," he answered. "This exercise is going to strengthen your back. Stop when you need to rest, but try it again. And each time, hold it just a little bit longer."

My immediate instinct was to stop when I first felt pain. I already didn't want to be there, and when I sensed an excuse I went for it. My self-protection instinct was fully engaged.

But the fitness instructor knew something I didn't. Or at least something I didn't want to admit: in order to get stronger, I *had to* experience the pain. I wished there was another way. I didn't want to feel discomfort. I wanted the end results without putting in the work.

That class was a perfect picture of how I face discomfort in most areas of my life. I'm sorry to admit that my instincts to avoid pain or discomfort have often kept me from achieving goals in my life. Maybe you've experienced this regret too. This happens partly because it's difficult to differentiate the pain we should avoid, like getting burned from touching a stove, and the kind of pain that makes us stronger. Pain just seems like pain—something to run from, something to avoid.

Which is why many of us find ourselves procrastinating on things that will cause us some measure of pain.

Pain seems to be a common side effect anytime we try to strengthen an area of our lives. And for most of us, that pain is emotional rather than physical. We avoid facing tasks, tackling projects, and addressing issues that are hard or would cause some measure of discomfort. As I mentioned before, it can be complicated to uncover the discomfort we are avoiding. But when I'm honest with myself, and do some digging, it's there.

Life Wasn't Meant to Be Easy

A big part of my procrastination problem stems from choosing ease over discomfort in most things. Yet I've come to understand and believe, in the deepest parts of myself, that life wasn't meant to be easy.

My previous view of life was to find ways to snuggle in where it's safe and to bring my family along with me. Minimize risks and play it smart. Find my comfort zone and stay there.

But that's not where Jesus is. When He came to earth, He didn't hide out where it was safe. He didn't choose His words carefully, trying to be politically correct. He didn't go where people expected Him to go or hang out with the "right" people. In fact, Jesus pretty much did the opposite of what people expected of Him. And none of it was "smart," "safe," or "comfortable."

So why were those things my life goals?

As hard as it is, I'm facing the weak parts of my life and character and realizing the only way to get stronger is to put myself in situations where it "hurts." There is no other way. The only way to strengthen muscles—and the only way to strengthen character and self-regulation—is to face resistance. Then face it again. And face it again.

Resistance Makes Us Stronger

As we dig deep into what we are resisting by procrastinating, it actually gets easier to press into the discomfort when we realize we are getting stronger.

By avoiding discomfort, I weaken my resolve. But by facing resistance, I strengthen it. The book *Born to Run* offers a brilliant example of how resistance actually makes us stronger. The author, Christopher McDougall, set out to discover why his foot hurt. It was a simple question that led him to the world of distance runners worldwide—from Tarahumara Indians in Mexico's Copper Canyons to Kenyans to American ultra-marathoners running hundreds of miles.

The journey was fascinating, even to this non-runner, as McDougall uncovered the biological reasons we were designed to run and how modern understanding and habits have changed that.

One eye-opening section focused on our feet and the revelation that human beings were designed to run without shoes. And the more shoe manufacturers have put support in their shoes, convincing us we need it, the weaker our feet and ankles have become.

McDougall interviewed a number of experts, one of them Dr. Gerald Hartmann, a physical therapist and expert on long-distance running. Hartmann said, "The deconditioned musculature of the foot is the greatest issue leading to injury, and we've allowed our feet to become badly deconditioned over the past twenty-five years." He continued, "Just look at the architecture. . . . Your foot's centerpiece is the arch, the greatest weight-bearing design ever created. The beauty of any arch is the way it gets stronger under stress; the harder you push down, the tighter its parts mesh. No stonemason worth his trowel would ever stick a support under an arch: push up from underneath, and you weaken the whole structure."[1]

When I read that, I had two huge *aha* moments. The first was a personal *aha*. Growing up in Phoenix, I went barefoot most of the year. And I've always worn flat sandals, even for a long day at an amusement park. For years my husband had told me I needed to wear tennis shoes. Finally, I was justified! In fact, I was almost giddy. You can imagine my joy at reading him section after section of that book.

The other *aha* moment applied to my continuing lesson of pressing in to what is most challenging in life: my personal search for ease has weakened my resolve when facing difficulty. It made so much sense. Just as we can weaken our feet and ankles by supporting them, we weaken our internal strength by avoiding resistance.

Here's the hard part: no one else can do this for us. We are the only ones who can strengthen our resolve and our self-regulation skills. And we do it by addressing our weak areas and facing them bravely.

The Bible has a promise for us when we discipline ourselves: "No discipline seems pleasant at the time, but painful. Later on, however, it produces a harvest of righteousness and peace for those who have been trained by it" (Heb. 12:11).

As I've faced my reasons for procrastinating, avoiding discipline plays a large part. Whether it's addressing a lifelong dream, forgiving someone who has hurt me, or cleaning my house when I'd rather be watching TV, life can be painful. I have to face potential hurt, discomfort, and challenge. However, when I consider that I'm getting stronger, it helps me push through many painful experiences in my life.

Plus, as a follower of Jesus, my life doesn't hold the promise of ease. In fact, it can contain quite the opposite. Much of what God asks me to do pushes me past my comfort zone. But the rewards, like the harvest of righteousness and peace mentioned in Hebrews 12, are powerful motivators.

Although our aversion to discomfort is a large reason behind why we procrastinate, it's not the only one. There are some significant cultural changes that have made it very difficult for women to get things done. One of the most challenging is the shift of responsibility in communication I mentioned briefly in the first chapter. I think it's worth understanding in greater depth.

Shift of Responsibility

When I was young, we had a house phone. Just one.

There was no answering machine or call waiting. So if you tried to call my mother and my sister was talking to a friend, you got a busy signal. So you tried again another time. In fact, you kept trying until someone answered. Or maybe you'd come over if it was important, or wait until your path crossed hers.

The burden to communicate was on the one with the need or the question. My, how times have changed.

With the advent of technology that keeps us interconnected in ways not imagined by generations before us, the burden to communicate has shifted. The weight of responsibility has passed from the communicator to the recipient dozens, if not hundreds, of times a day.

Now you email me and it's my job to respond.

You text me, and I had better text back.

Every day there are people wanting to communicate with me. And they happily pass the ball to me and wait. Through emails, texts, phone calls, private messages, and social media, communication bombards my day and redirects my attention.

This daily avalanche of information and input drastically impacts our ability to get things done. As our lives are increasingly open to input from others, it's getting harder to identify our priorities.

I might start the day with a clear plan for what I want to accomplish, when a ding interrupts my thoughts. I know I should just keep working, but then my phone dings again. (It's like my phone nags me if I don't immediately check the new text.) Reading the text, I see it's a message from a coworker who asks if I've seen the email she just sent me.

Putting my project aside, I respond to her text, letting her know I'll look now. Then I open my email to respond. As I do, I see twelve more emails have arrived. And they aren't junk mail.

The priorities that seemed so clear just minutes prior are now muddy. What should I do? Return to the project? Answer the emails?

This is just a snapshot of what happens in our homes and offices every day. People's expectation of a prompt response is increasing. We're becoming more impatient with delays, especially when we want an answer.

As our interconnectedness increases, this shift in responsibility to communicate is making us reactive rather than proactive. Which greatly affects our ability to manage our workload and get things done in a timely fashion.

The more my life is directed by the demands of others, the less able I am to manage my responsibilities. And not only manage them but even identify them.

When I objectively evaluate the demands on my time, it becomes obvious that I spend the best parts of my day on other people's priorities. True, I do have people I choose to give my time and energy to—I'm a wife, mother, and employee. These are assignments given to me by God, and there are people whose needs are joyfully my priority.

But that's not what I'm talking about. I'm referring to the needs and questions that don't have to be responded to immediately. Even from those people whom I love the most. There are even some demands that aren't mine to handle but my high sense of responsibility prompts me to react.

For most of us, it is ingrained to respond immediately. We can picture the person who texted us watching their phone for a response. Hence the number of us with phones at the ready all hours of the day.

People-Pleasing Problems

This reactionary approach to life is a problem we must address if we are going to face the issue of procrastination and over-loaded schedules. The solution is empowering and simple, but very hard for those who struggle with people-pleasing. Most of us don't want to offend others, and this need to please at times drives us to make poor choices, choices that negatively impact our priorities.

Lysa TerKeurst, author of *The Best Yes*, puts it this way: "We are afraid of people not liking us. Not admiring us. Not being pleased with us. So we spend the best of who we are doing a million things we know we aren't supposed to be doing."[2]

While there are always demanding people in our lives, sometimes the most unrealistic demands come from inside our own heads. Many times I've twisted myself into knots trying to achieve what I thought someone wanted, only to realize they didn't have such high expectations after all.

My deepest fear when it comes to people-pleasing is that others will think I'm not capable. I so want to do things right and for others to respect my work that I will spend the best parts of myself on projects for other people and neglect my personal goals and priorities.

We Struggle to Identify Our True Priorities

Honestly, as my life becomes more interconnected with others, these others have more opportunities to speak into my life, and it's getting harder even to figure out exactly what those priorities are. Am I supposed to stay focused on my work, or stop it to help you? I think of the story of the good Samaritan found in Luke 10, where Jesus honors the one who put aside his agenda to help another. But that help met a very significant need.

There will always be new demands rising to the top of our to-do list, giving us a reason to delay tackling our own agenda. Some women are so used to helping others they don't even know what God's priorities are for them.

I'm always having to rein myself in and reevaluate my priorities. In fact, I do this weekly, and I'll explain that more in a later chapter. But for now, perhaps a series of questions I ask myself will help you if you struggle with knowing your priorities. These would be good questions to write in a journal or notebook and answer during the next week. To answer them effectively, take time to pray before you start. Open your heart to hear the Lord and His voice. Quiet your heart and just listen. Then ask yourself:

1) What Can Only I Do?

There are some jobs in my life no one else can do. For example, no one else can nurture my personal faith in God. I am the only wife my husband has. God has given me five children to mother. Plus, no one else can eat the right foods or exercise for me. Those four areas of life (plus a few others) are no-brainers and will always be at the top of my priority list.

2) What Has God Entrusted to Me?

We've all been entrusted with something—a certain amount of money, a home, talents, and intelligence. Some of us have paid jobs and volunteer responsibilities.

3) Am I a Good Steward of What I Already Have?

This is where I do a painful assessment of reality. How am I doing with what God has already given me? Are my finances a wreck? Have I neglected my husband? Have I honored my parents? God is always watching to see how I'm doing with what He's already given me. When He sees I manage things well, He entrusts me with more. When I'm neglectful, the opposite happens.

4) What Passion (or Dream) Has God Put in My Heart?

Perhaps this dream is buried in your heart—but it's there. When we submit to God's plan for our lives, and those dreams don't contradict His Word or character, we can be confident God placed those dreams in our heart for a reason.

5) What Has God Asked Me to Do That I Haven't Done Yet?

This is where things get touchy for a procrastinator. It's likely there are items we've put off that God has called us to do. This moves our procrastination into the realm of disobedience.

I once heard this statement: "Old orders are standing orders." Meaning if God asked you to do something years ago, and didn't revise the directions, He still expects you to do it. It's never too late to be obedient.

Overwhelmed and Overloaded

Another reason many of us procrastinate is overload. We simply can't do it all. It's not that we are lazy. Many women bothered by procrastination are productive in most areas of their lives. They love making lists and checking things off. They are accomplishment-oriented.

And the need to achieve is strong.

So when faced with the choice between an easy accomplishment (and another item checked off a to-do list) or a harder, more demanding task (something that would require facing a weakness), we take the easier route, thereby satisfying that achievement need.

The need to achieve can lead us to our best work or busywork. The challenge is knowing which is which. And that is where we must depend on God to give us direction.

I've met some women who are highly successful in business and yet can't seem to get things done around the house. I've also met women who are wildly creative and can pull off the most beautiful birthday party or wedding shower and yet can't get their taxes done on time.

When we are accomplished in an area of our lives, it's easy to make an excuse for why we neglect other parts. We're busy, after all. If that were the only reason things didn't get done, solving the problem would be easy. We could all just do less.

Yet no matter how much we get done, in the quiet of the evening, after the rush of the day is over, productive women are acutely aware of what *didn't* get done. This discontent over our lack of accomplishments is linked to another characteristic for those with a need to achieve: high personal expectations. Too high, most times.

And the combination of high achieving and high expectations creates a confusing mix of emotions. My happiness and joy over completing tasks are almost always tempered by feelings of dissatisfaction. It's difficult to ever feel a sense of completion because there's so much left to do. Or I think I should have done things better.

I'm plagued by the word *but*. Yes, I pulled off a nice dinner, but I should have made a different entrée. I organized my closet, but I wish I had done a better job with my shoes. I planned that vacation with my mom, but I wish I had done more research on restaurants in the cities we visited.

Then, like a taunt, self-defeating thoughts enter my mind:

You don't have what it takes.
You'll never accomplish that.
You may try, but you'll never measure up.

No one would ever know I struggle with those thoughts, because on the surface I look productive.

These thoughts don't come from a childhood of disapproval. They don't come from a litany of criticism over the years. I'm thankful to have grown up with a mother who believed in me and spoke possibility into my life. And although my father wasn't emotionally involved in my life, he didn't speak critical words.

No, all that disappointment comes from within. I'm wired to produce and achieve, and when that doesn't happen to my expectations I doubt myself.

Procrastination is a complex issue, with many possible causes. My hope is that as you start to address some of the reasons why you delay doing what's best, you'll have some *aha* moments that will help you change.

● PRACTICAL APPLICATION

One of the key topics in this chapter is the idea of resistance making us stronger. When we press into the challenging parts of life, we are actually getting stronger. You may not experience immediate change, but over time you will see improvement.

Consider those two things you'd like to change. If you consistently faced what causes you discomfort in these areas, what would grow stronger? What skills would you develop? How would your internal character change?

My regular task:

My personal goal:

4

Assessing the Price We Pay

Most of us are cost-conscious. Few have unlimited income, so we shop sales, watch for flight prices to drop, and do crazy things like face Black Friday crowds.

My kids say I'm cheap, but I prefer the term *thrifty*. When you grow up with modest means, you learn to stretch a dollar. My family was expert at recycling before going green was hip.

So I am very aware of the cost of most things. Except my choices.

I know down to the penny how much my latte will cost, how much movie tickets cost (a ridiculous amount), and when chicken is a bargain. But the cost of the decisions I make? Not so much.

In fact, I tend to forget there is a price to pay for every decision. Sometimes I get so focused on what I need or want to do in the moment, that I miss the big picture. I miss the interconnectivity of my decisions and underestimate the impact of little choices. But every yes to one choice is actually also a no to something else.

The Price of Good Decisions

This is how life works, but so often we operate outside that reality. Then we are surprised when plans don't go according to our expectations.

Here's an example of what I mean. If I say yes to reading my Bible every day, then I have to say no to the morning news or a favorite novel. I might have to say no to sleeping in thirty more minutes or to staying up late and watching another show.

To accomplish my goal of daily Bible reading, there will be a cost.

If I say yes to giving to a local mission project every month, I'm saying no to going out to eat, or whatever else I would have purchased with that money.

Because we don't have unlimited time, energy, and money, what we say no to is part of the cost of every decision. Jesus communicated the importance of considering the cost of our decisions. Specifically, He challenged people to consider the cost of following Him:

> Large crowds were traveling with Jesus, and turning to them he said: "If anyone comes to me and does not hate father and mother, wife and children, brothers and sisters—yes, even their own life—such a person cannot be my disciple. And whoever does not carry their cross and follow me cannot be my disciple.
>
> "Suppose one of you wants to build a tower. Won't you first sit down and estimate the cost to see if you have enough money to complete it? For if you lay the foundation and are not able to finish it, everyone who sees it will ridicule you, saying, 'This person began to build and wasn't able to finish.'" (Luke 14:25–30)

I wonder if Jesus looked over the "large crowds" and knew that many of them would start following Him with the greatest intentions. They would get caught up in the excitement of a new rabbi, one who performed miracles at that. I imagine His heart burst with longing for these lost sheep to trust Him as their shepherd, yet He knew their hearts would easily be led astray.

Jesus knew how high the cost to follow Him would be. He knew His disciples would face ridicule, rejection, persecution, and death. And yet this teaching shows He believed that by counting the cost ahead of time, His followers would be better able to stand firm when things got tough.

It matters to Jesus that we finish what we start. And it matters that others will look at our lives and see how well we follow through on our commitments. And one way we finish well is to count the cost of our choices.

The Cost of Bad Decisions

Once we acknowledge there's a cost to every decision, it's actually easier to count the cost of good ones. If we want to be a sincere follower of Jesus, we're going to have to put Him first in our lives. If we want a college degree, we're going to have to work hard, spend a lot of money, and be poor while we are students.

But what about the cost of poor decisions? Well, those aren't quite so easy to identify. Oh, some are easy—speed and you get a ticket. But sometimes it's harder to see the connection between our bad choices and the cost of those choices.

For example, when we make a bad decision to sleep late on a workday, we're saying no to a peaceful morning. The cost of that choice is a stressful, impatient morning. It might include arriving late to work, or forgetting to take an important document along.

The same thing happens when we procrastinate. There is always a price to pay. Sometimes we pay it. Sometimes others pay it. But there is a cost. If we want to make wiser decisions, we must be honest about this reality and factor in the cost of our choices. Otherwise we are at a disadvantage. We will never reach our goals or accomplish what's most important to us, and we'll be surprised and disappointed yet again.

Let me put it another way: when we ignore the cost of our choices, we are deceived. And deceived is just where our enemy wants us to stay. You see, Satan is an expert at hiding the cost of our choices. He doesn't want us to know there will be any negative consequences. If we do see the consequences, he wants us to think they are insignificant and barely impact those around us.

But what he really wants is for us to think we slipped past the consequences: no harm, no foul. *So go ahead and relax*, the lying enemy whispers. *There's no harm in starting tomorrow*. Since we already struggle with guilt, we want to believe that lie. It makes it much easier to justify our choices.

The reason this deception works is that the cost of procrastination is often delayed. Its impact adds up slowly, so it's hard to define or measure until it's obvious, painful, and expensive. Let's address some of the most common costs of procrastination, because I believe when we are able to count the cost in advance, we are better able to stand strong under the temptation to put off till tomorrow what we should do today.

Some costs are external, like money wasted when we miss a warranty deadline. But I think God cares most about the internal costs. So let's start with one that's painful to admit, hard to address, but critically important as we become godly women.

The Cost to Our Character

As a young college graduate with a degree in journalism and public relations, my first job was at a land development office. It was a start-up company and I was given a hybrid position. It included marketing and writing, which I loved, and answering the phones, which I didn't love. The owners promised my position would develop as the company expanded.

So I took the job, happy to have it.

One of my bosses was a woman with a very strong personality. She was smart, confident, and aggressive. And very successful. She was also one of those people who never forgets a thing and had high expectations for herself and her employees.

Over time, both the company and my work level grew . . . but I still answered the phones. Eventually, it got to the point where I wasn't managing things very well. I'd get great assignments and be excited to start, but then reality would step in and I'd be overwhelmed. Rather than tackling those big projects right away, I put them off, finding it easier to work on simpler things.

My boss was very hands-on and often called me into her office for an update on my projects. I found myself dreading those meetings, knowing she'd be displeased with my lack of progress. I could feel myself getting anxious as I fell further behind. And that is when the lies started.

"Yes, that project is coming along nicely." "I'm almost finished." "I'm just waiting for a few more pieces of information."

After those meetings, I'd rush back to my desk and frantically try to make my progress match the inaccurate response I'd just given. At first I justified my replies as "half-truths." Perhaps they were, if statements like "coming along nicely" and "almost finished" meant "I'm thinking about starting anytime now."

Over time, the lies and truth became jumbled. Rather than face my procrastination for what it was, I always found something convenient to blame. The truth was, I was overwhelmed and put off hard projects.

I'd crossed a line of personal integrity that nagged at the edges of my conscience, but I felt helpless to change. Until one day my boss gave me another request: lie for her.

She hadn't gotten something done and asked me to give false information if a certain person called while she was out. She left the office and I felt sick to my stomach. This wasn't right. She hadn't even started the project. And now I was supposed to cover for her? It was as if God made me do a 180 and stare at the line of integrity I had already crossed.

I'd compromised my character one excuse, one rationalization, one lie at a time. It was an incredibly hard decision for me, but when my boss returned to the office, I told her I wouldn't lie for her.

God used that experience to show me that my character is far more important to Him than my career. Since that day, I've challenged myself to be completely honest with others about my progress on things I say I'll do.

It's so easy for lies, justification, and blame to bubble up to the surface and tickle my tongue. I so desperately want others to think I'm capable that excuses and dishonesty could easily become a habit. But just like exercise makes me physically stronger, choosing to tell the truth develops my character. Every time.

Telling the truth also serves as a method of accountability for me. Others don't know they are helping keep me accountable, but when I know I'm going to tell them the truth, it motivates me to get going.

Plus, it's freeing to be able to say, "Hey, I'm really sorry I haven't gotten started. It's something I struggle with." As much as I don't like admitting weakness, people are drawn more to humility than prideful dishonesty. Rather than diminish their respect, I've found being honest and humble actually increases it.

Interestingly, the stronger my character gets, the stronger my abilities are too.

The Cost to Our Calling

Another cost of procrastination happens when we delay or abandon the calling God puts on our lives.

People talk about God's "call" on their lives, and that can mean different things. Usually it means a big commitment of time, energy, or money. Like deciding to homeschool or choosing a certain career path. God's calling can change with our seasons of life, or it can be something we live with our entire lives.

Sometimes we *know* God is calling us to do something, but we drag our heels. Our heads and hearts are filled with excuses . . . *I'm too young, too old, too busy, not qualified.*

And since God's call on our lives almost always involves a challenge, for those of us who struggle with procrastination this call can seem daunting. So we drag our feet some more.

It was 2004 when I felt God's call to write a book. I could feel passion burn in my heart. I just *knew* I was supposed to write. So I started praying about what kind of book I was supposed to write. Finally, I had an idea.

Excitedly, I shared my book idea with a friend and her response doused my dream with cold water. "Aren't there lots of books out there on that topic?" she asked. And not long after that conversation, my excuses started: *I'm not good enough. I don't have anything new to write about. Others are better than me.*

That was all it took. So I put off my plans to write. Stopped talking about it. Filed my notes in a drawer. And stuffed down the dream God had planted in my heart.

Until one day, two years later, a question brought it back to life. At the end of church one Sunday, the pastor ended his sermon with this statement: "God has asked some of you to do something, and you haven't done it yet."

My heart started pounding as adrenaline surged through my veins. He was talking about me. I headed up to the front of the church for prayer that day and confessed my disobedience.

I realized God hadn't asked me to manage the results of my obedience, just to be obedient to His call on my life. I did write that book.

And I found a publisher a year later who published the book the year after that. And it went out of print within eighteen months.

Obviously this isn't the Hallmark movie ending. It would be so much more dramatic if I could tell you that book went on to be a bestseller. However, by being obedient to that call to write, delayed as it was, I was able to see God open up more opportunities for me to write in the years to follow.

I wish I had answered God's calling right away. I missed out on two years of walking in obedience in this area of my life and the joy of serving Him in writing. I'll also never know what might have happened had I written that book earlier.

What is God calling you to do that you haven't done yet? It's never too late to obey. Don't worry about the results, just leave those to God. I'm convinced God will be pleased with your obedience.

The Cost of Unmet Potential

Many of us live with the sadness of unmet potential. Our histories are a résumé of unfulfilled dreams, unfinished projects, and missed opportunities.

"If onlys" litter our past. We know we could have done better *if only* we'd started earlier, not rushed, or given up in exasperation.

In what areas could we have found success? What excellence could we have discovered in ourselves if we did the work like we planned at the start? What would have happened had we worked diligently on our goals, faithfully, rather than in spurts of effort?

We know our best work is untapped when we procrastinate, and that knowledge is a constant companion. The cost of our unmet potential is immeasurable; the regret is heavy.

The need to believe we have potential is something we never outgrow. It's what makes us feel needed. It's something we long for others to see in us our entire lives.

Although others might not see our potential, and we might miss it ourselves, God has a vision for us that is untainted by past performance. He knows what is possible for us, and He does not give up on us. In fact, God steps in to offer His help when we are weak.

What potential is locked in you? Have you given up on yourself? If so, please know your potential is brand-new every day in Christ. Allow Him to give you a vision for who you can become and what you can do.

Liberty Savard, in her book *Shattering Your Strongholds*, says this about God's vision for us:

> Only with God can you start over more than once with an unblemished, untarnished, 100 percent, still-intact potential . . . the same potential He has always intended you to fulfill.[1]

Without a vision for our potential, we can feel hopeless to ever achieve anything of substance. In fact, procrastination can make us feel like bystanders in our own lives—always on the sidelines. While God is the Author of our lives, we must make a deep commitment to stewarding our stories. We can start by acknowledging that procrastination has robbed many of us of our potential and embrace God's invitation to try again.

The Cost to Our Health

Procrastination isn't an obvious thief of our health. It's not like ingesting poison. Rather, its effects are usually only seen in hindsight.

One of the things most women procrastinate on is exercise. We know we should do it. We read statistics that tell us we can reduce our risk of breast cancer by 50 percent if we exercise. We know it will help us get to a healthy weight. Weight-bearing exercise will build strong bones, which we'll need as we get older. And the benefits go on and on.

As do the excuses. We plan to sign up for an exercise class but don't know the times. We talk about meeting a friend at the gym but can't get it scheduled. We'd go for a walk but it's too dark.

We also know we should eat better. But we've delayed so long on a project due the next day that we stay late at work and pick up fast food on the way home. Or we neglect to take the time to make a weekly menu, because that would involve looking at recipes and comparing the sales, and who has time for that? So rather than planning a healthy meal, we find it's easier to grab something packaged or frozen.

Sound familiar? These types of choices add up over time. And before you know it, your doctor says you have high blood pressure. Or your blood test is showing higher than normal levels of something.

A more direct effect of procrastination on our health is putting off screenings or dealing with potential risks. For example, no one wants to go get the "girls" smashed. But depending on your age, a mammogram can reduce your risks of dying from breast cancer up to 35 percent.[1] And as we get older, there are more "fun" screenings we get to address.

Another hidden health risk of procrastination is the cumulative effects of stress. Chronic procrastination means chronic stress. When our bodies are under stress, our fight-or-flight response activates. Our hypothalamus triggers an alarm system, which sets off a series of automatic reactions designed to provide energy to react. Our bodies give us a shot of adrenaline and cortisol, which increase our heart rate and raise our blood pressure. We are poised to do what's necessary to save our lives.

This process happens occasionally in a person whose life is balanced. And afterward, their body returns to a healthy state of rest. But a person who lives with chronic procrastination, and one pressing deadline after another, will experience overexposure to these stress hormones, causing all sorts of havoc to their body, including:

Anxiety

Depression

Digestive problems

Heart disease

Sleep problems

Weight gain

Memory and concentration impairment[3]

When our health is good, it's easy to procrastinate. But as I mentioned before, we are stewards of our story. Being proactive with our health makes a profound difference in our quality of life and our ability to live out our God-given potential.

The High Cost of Procrastination

There are so many other costs of procrastination. We can experience financial costs by accruing late fees, missing warranty deadlines, and failing to return unwanted items by the refund date. In our rush to finish projects, we can produce a lower quality of work and make more mistakes. Our relationships suffer when we delay dealing with issues or impose extra work on others because of our last-minute efforts. Procrastination isn't harmless. There are so many more costs than I've mentioned here. And I would much rather jump right to the solutions—but I need to make sure you understand what price you are paying if you continue procrastinating.

Probably the greatest cost any of us can pay is in our relationships. First with God, then with those we love. Delaying a

commitment to follow Jesus can come with an eternal conse-
quence. And delaying investing in relationships can come with
lifelong regrets. One of my biggest regrets is that I thought I would
have more time with my sister.

She was diagnosed with breast cancer in 2011 and decided to
aggressively respond by undergoing a mastectomy. Sadly, the cancer was also found in a few lymph nodes. Her optimism carried
her through the difficult treatments, and after completing chemo
she returned to good health.

It was six months after chemotherapy had ended when she told
us that the doctors had found a spot on her lungs and she was
preparing for surgery again. We lived in neighboring states, which
made the drive doable. But my busy schedule with kids and work
hindered the number of times I went to see her. Something always
came up and I'd put it off.

My sister was positive, and I wanted to be positive too. So her
graciousness and optimism eased my conscience. I was able to
make a few trips, but nothing like I wanted to. The final trip I made
was to be there during her lung surgery. Only they canceled it that
morning. Sadly, I wasn't able to return when she actually had surgery. I told her I'd be over to see her soon, but one week slipped
into another and I didn't go.

She was doing fairly well after that second surgery, until weeks
later she complained of a backache. She thought she pulled something when she was cleaning. A heating pad, massages, and pain
medication barely helped. In a matter of days, her speech was
slurred and she was confused. Our concern immediately shot up,
but before we could even plan a trip, she was hospitalized and
unresponsive. The disease had silently spread, and two weeks later
she was gone.

If only I could turn back time as easy as flipping the pages on
a calendar. My priorities would have been obvious. I would have

rescheduled work and volunteer responsibilities. Signed my kids out of school and taken them with me. Set aside everything that really didn't matter in light of the opportunity to spend one more day with my sister.

But I can't. I can only pray for God's help in not making those same choices again. Late payments and cluttered homes are annoying, but they can be dealt with in time. People have an expiration date—we just don't know when it is.

To live with fewer regrets, we must come face-to-face with our procrastination and overloaded lives. And we must prioritize God and people over everything. May I encourage you to put down this book and call someone you love? You'll be glad you did.

● PRACTICAL APPLICATION

Some of the costs of procrastination are minor—and others much more expensive. As you consider those two areas you want to change, what are the costs you pay by not attending to them? I detailed five areas of cost in this chapter: character, calling, unmet potential, health, and relationships. There are many more, like loss of peace, disorder, hurry, and disobedience to God.

The price I pay by not managing my regular task well is:

The price I pay by not pursuing my personal goal is:

5

Myth Busters

I *work better under pressure!*

Maybe you haven't *spoken* these words, but have you *thought* them? Most of us have. There is something about the last minute that motivates us to work harder. And there's nothing like an approaching deadline to light a fire under us.

But do we really work better under pressure? Well, that's somewhat of a myth. In fact, there are a number of myths about procrastination. Maybe you've believed some of these yourself:

I'll feel more like it tomorrow.

I'm too busy to get that done.

I'll have more time next week.

I'll get some easy things done and work my way up to the hard stuff.

I can do this all by myself, I just need more time.

These sound so realistic and logical. On the surface, they seem true. And who would argue with you? If you said any of these statements to a friend, she would nod her head in agreement.

However, each of these statements has a problem. They are all based on a faulty foundation. We really don't work *better* under pressure. We won't *ever* feel like doing certain things. And when we're honest, we know we won't have more time next week.

When we take the time to unpack each of these beliefs, we'll find they are all more like urban legends than reality.

To address procrastination at its root, we must start with our thoughts, which in turn affect our beliefs, ultimately influencing our behavior. Maybe you've already figured this out, but procrastinators are wishful thinkers. We live in this lovely fairy-tale world where things will always work out and unpleasant tasks will certainly be easier tomorrow.

And too often we base our actions on truth that isn't really true. Which leads us to procrastination and all the problems that causes in our lives.

Maybe you'd rather believe these statements. And if so, I should have put this chapter at the end. That way if you get annoyed at me for removing some mental crutches, you'll have already read the rest of the book. But hopefully you are ready to make some changes in your life and are open to some myth busting. If so, let's start with a biggie.

"I Work Better under Pressure"

Perhaps you've felt the rush of adrenaline to meet a deadline. It can be exhilarating. Your mind finally feels focused, your energy level is high, and you might even enjoy doing the work. But very few, if any, of us are glad we waited until the last minute. In fact, it's likely that in the midst of the panicked rush we wonder why we waited so long to get started, because the actual task wasn't as bad as our dreading of it.

The idea that we work *better* under pressure is a myth we tell ourselves to justify our delay. As with many myths, this one gets its start in some truth, with a helpful hormone called adrenaline.

Adrenaline is a stress hormone released from the adrenal glands above our kidneys when we are afraid, angry, or excited.[1] It's God's gift of energy to prepare us for action. If you've ever slammed on your brakes and barely missed getting into an accident, you've probably felt it surge through your body. This is an adrenalin rush.

An adrenaline rush can be very helpful when facing the stress of an approaching deadline. On the surface, we might think we are working better under the pressure. The truth is, some people need the stress of an approaching deadline to just *do* the work.

Working "better" requires time for most of us. Time allows us to think without pressure. When we're at deadline, deep processing is an extravagance. In our rush to finish, our results will be superficial and lacking richness and depth. Depending on the severity of the consequences of missing the deadline, sometimes we can't think clearly at all.

This is because that same adrenaline rush infusing us with energy has a side effect. It hinders our executive processing, which makes it hard for us to problem-solve, thereby compromising the quality of our work.

Researchers at Yale University have studied the brain's response to stress and have uncovered the detrimental effect of stress hormones on the prefrontal cortex, where our executive processing happens. When life is calm, the prefrontal cortex acts as the manager of our brain, overseeing and solving problems and keeping our emotions under control. However, it doesn't take much to upset this delicate balance of mental processing and emotional response: "Under even everyday stresses, the prefrontal cortex can shut down, allowing the amygdala, a locus for regulating emotional activity, to take over, inducing mental paralysis and panic."[2]

When faced with stress, we won't be operating at our best. You might be wondering why God would design this "weakness" into our response. And I did too. Why not make our focus sharper when faced with stress? That seems more logical. And helpful.

But after considering it, and knowing that our God is kind and loves us greatly, I believe this response was designed to save our lives in the face of danger.

Perhaps God knows that when we are face-to-face with a hungry lion, it is not the time for us to stand our ground, trying to reason our way out of it. If we stood there trying to consider the speed at which the lion could run, how high it could climb a tree, when it might have had its last meal, and what other prey we could distract it with, we'd be dead.

We simply need to have the energy to run or drop to the ground and play dead.

So how do we deal with this limitation? Some professionals are trained to deal with stress. I can't imagine a professional quarterback or a Navy SEAL running away or freezing whenever they are in danger. Although it certainly has happened, they wouldn't last long in their chosen profession. All those who knowingly face pressure of the highest kind train, train, and then train some more, until habit takes over.

Should that be our response? Should we train ourselves to deal with the pressure of procrastination by procrastinating more? Probably not. Rather, we should protect our touchy prefrontal cortex by building in time for calm consideration. And look for ways to avoid the stress of the last minute.

When I work under pressure, I will get the job done but my results will be only adequate, a shadow of what I could do with time. That's not the type of work I want to produce, nor is it the type of work God wants me to produce. Brian Tracy, author of *Eat That Frog!*, says, "Under the pressure of deadlines, often self-created through procrastination, people suffer greater stress, make more mistakes, and have to redo more tasks than under any other condition."[3]

Doing our best work is a spiritual practice; the Bible says everything we do is for the Lord. "Whatever you do, work at it with all your heart, as working for the Lord, not for human masters, since you know that you will receive an inheritance from the Lord as a reward. It is the Lord Christ you are serving" (Col. 3:23–24).

"I'll Feel More Like It Tomorrow"

Tomorrow is full of promise. Tomorrow we will be motivated to start our diet, look for a new job, apply for a loan, or practice the piano. Only when tomorrow becomes today, we realize we feel the same way. And so the cycle starts again as we plan for yet another tomorrow.

The danger for us is we derive a certain satisfaction from just thinking about starting on our goals. Amazingly, we don't actually have to start working on them to feel better. Timothy Pychyl, PhD, author of *Solving the Procrastination Puzzle*, puts it this way, "There is nothing like a righteous intention now for an action later to make us feel good."[4]

Why do we think we'll be more motivated tomorrow than we are today? Probably because we have an inaccurate forecast of our own motivation. This is why so many of us make New Year's resolutions only to struggle to live them out.

Josh Riebock, in his book *Heroes and Monsters*, says, "Everyone can change tomorrow. Everyone solves problems tomorrow. But the only changes that matter are the ones I make today. Tomorrow is the easiest day I'll ever live. Today is the scary one, which is probably why I've spent so much time avoiding it."[5]

It's self-defeating to believe we need our emotions in alignment with our goals. There are some things we will never "feel" like doing, but we do them anyway. Our emotions are undependable.

In fact the Bible says it this way: "The heart is deceitful above all things and beyond cure. Who can understand it?" (Jer. 17:9).

The ancients understood the "heart" to be not only the seat of all our emotions but also our thoughts. They knew what we sometimes forget, that it's not always wise to be ruled by our hearts. Sometimes our hearts lead us astray.

This idea conflicts with much of modern thought, where "following your heart" is desirable. It's not so popular to train ourselves to do what's right despite what our hearts say. But that's exactly what we need to do to overcome procrastination and an overlong to-do list.

A wise and loving parent trains children to do things they don't feel like doing, such as get along with siblings, clean up after themselves, and do their homework. Very few children are born with the motivation to act in selfless ways. Few say, "Brother, please take my toys!" or "I'd love to clean up my room before going out to play." By teaching them responsibility, we raise children to be mature adults. We train them to do the right thing, and hopefully the benefits are positive enough to reinforce the behavior.

Perhaps we need to return to this model of training for ourselves, in order to do what's right in spite of how we feel.

Successful people know that motivation often comes *after* starting the project. Creativity comes once we sit down at the keyboard. Passion flourishes once we begin. Progress, even small amounts, fuels motivation, creativity, passion, and productivity.

One of my college-age children recently came to me and said, "Thank you for making us pull weeds. It has helped me do the things I know I need to do."

The next time you don't feel like doing something, remind yourself that you won't feel like it tomorrow either, so just start. Today.

"I'm Too Busy to Get That Done"

Personally, I don't think being busy is bad. But being overbusy most definitely is. And I've dedicated an entire chapter to this topic of being too busy, but for now, let's just admit something together: *We are never too busy for what we really want to do.*

There are some extreme exceptions to this, and I don't want to discount the woman who is in a season of life where her time really isn't her own. But that's not true for everyone. Most of us have a certain amount of flexible time in our days. We have choices of how we spend that time, and we live with the consequences of our choices.

The reality is we have the ability to make changes in our schedules and how we spend our time. And very often we can find time when we are motivated to do something. Sometimes I have to admit that it's not *really* an issue of busyness but of my own delay. And when I get to that place of honesty, I can start to address the issue.

"I've Got This!"

Sometimes our independent natures lead us to procrastinate. Rather than accept help or delegate work, we fiercely hold on to things we should release. Sometimes it's a control issue; other times it's a need to be respected. And then there are times when we've misplaced our trust by putting it in ourselves rather than in God.

It's a myth to think we can do everything well. We weren't created to always work in isolation. We were meant to live interconnected lives, which is why we are all given different strengths. When we ignore this truth, it can lead us down roads of procrastination.

I recently took on a project at work I thought I could handle. I knew I could organize it, categorize it, and present it to my coworkers. But I didn't have any idea how to present it to the public. How would we put it on the website? Where would it go? How would the user access the information? I was stumped.

This project was assigned to me in April, but rather than asking for help I moved it from one to-do list to another. My summer got busy organizing our annual writer's and speaker's conference, and I had a handy excuse for procrastinating.

Finally, after the conference in August, I had no more excuses. Others were waiting on me to do my part, which was holding up the entire project. Finally, I confessed at a meeting that I couldn't even get started because I couldn't figure out the final technology piece. Immediately, a member of my team spoke up and said, "Don't worry about that, I'll figure it out. Just get me your information."

With that offer of help, I had my part done in a week.

My independence can be a serious weakness that hinders me in getting things done. Although I'll stop what I'm doing to help others, I prefer to do most things myself.

For so many years, a desperation to appear qualified drove me to take on tasks and responsibilities that were outside my strengths and were unrealistic given my available time and resources. Rather than pray about my decisions I pressed on, confident in my own abilities.

It took a move across the country and giving up my job and volunteer leadership roles at church for me to see truth: my sense of worth and value were directly connected to *my* accomplishments. That's what led me to take on more than I should have and try to prove my qualifications. When no one knew what I could do, I felt like a failure.

That was the start of God rebuilding the foundation of my identity. He started teaching me that my true worth would never be found in what I did, only in who I was: His child.

When you've measured your worth by your achievements, it's hard to release those expectations. But I'm learning that I don't have to prove myself. And despite my superwoman complex, which got me into all kinds of situations, I'm not able to do *all* things.

In fact it's freeing to admit there's much more I *can't* do well than I *can* do well.

The older I get, the more I realize that in order to play to my strengths, I've got to be okay with my weaknesses. Plus, there's something beautiful that happens when I admit I need help: others get to use their strengths. Then when we all bring our best, we create a dream team.

When I eliminate things I don't do well from my to-do list, it's amazing how much easier it is to start. Seriously, the last thing I want to tackle is something I *know* I stink at. But when I work in a sweet spot, it's amazing how motivated I am.

But there's another independence that's dangerous. And that's believing I don't need God. Well, let me clarify. In my head I know I need God, but sometimes in my daily life I go about my business thinking I'll call God when I'm in trouble, but until then, *I've got this.*

God calls this *pride*, and here's what His Word says about it:

"In his pride the wicked man does not seek him; in all his thoughts there is no room for God." (Ps. 10:4)

"When pride comes, then comes disgrace, but with humility comes wisdom." (Prov. 11:2)

"Pride goes before destruction, a haughty spirit before a fall." (Prov. 16:18)

Just like we were designed to live *interdependent* with each other, we were also created to live *dependent* on God. God doesn't want us living apart from Him. He wants to be actively involved in our lives, giving us wisdom for decisions and power to face our challenges.

There's a story in the Old Testament that illustrates God's desire for us to depend on Him. It's the story of Gideon facing the Midianites. Early in the morning, Gideon and 32,000 warriors prepared for battle against an army of at least 135,000 (see Judges). Gideon's men were seriously outnumbered.

But God was preparing to demonstrate His power and protection over His children. So in Judges 7:2, the Lord said to Gideon, "You have too many men. I cannot deliver Midian into their hands, or Israel would boast against me, 'My own strength has saved me.'"

God then told Gideon to send home anyone who trembled with fear, and 22,000 men left. Then God told Gideon to take the men to a water source and separate those who lapped the water with their tongues from those who got down on their knees to drink. Three hundred men lapped the water from cupped hands. The rest were sent home.

God whittled Gideon's army down to three hundred men. Then, and only then, did God tell Gideon to enter into the battle. Gideon attacked the Midianite camp, and with God's strength he and his men were victorious.

God wants to give us His strength for the work we have to do. He wants to direct our paths and be our encourager. But He can't do that when we shut Him out. God is tearing down my independence, brick by brick, and I'm so glad.

Myths can be fun to tell in a children's story, but they are detrimental when dealing with procrastination. What other myths might you believe? Take the time to consider if they are helping you complete your best work—or if they are hurting you.

● PRACTICAL APPLICATION

It's easy to justify putting things off. But true procrastination involves a voluntary delay of something we could do but choose not to. So we've got to remove those crutches that have been keeping us from moving forward.

As you consider the two goals you set at the beginning of the book, are there any "myths" that are hindering your completion of them? To begin to master your workload and goals, try to identify what false reasons might be hindering you.

Myths I tell myself . . .

About my regular task:

About my personal goal:

6

Overcoming Our Fears

A hero is no braver than an ordinary man, but he is brave five minutes longer.

Ralph Waldo Emerson

My elementary school campus was divided between lower and upper grades. First through fourth composed the lower grades, and fifth through eighth the upper grades. Not only was there an age difference but the upper grades also had separate buildings and a separate playground, rotated between classes, and ate a later lunch. As the start of fifth grade approached, my anxiety level increased. I was afraid of everything about fifth grade. I was worried how I would wait another hour to eat and what it would be like with all the "big kids." I was a wreck. On the first day of school, I was so sick with fear I ended up in the nurse's office.

One day later I was fine. All those unknowns of fifth grade had become known and I was no longer a quivering mess.

Fear of change and the unknown has kept me from doing many things in my life. Thankfully God has brought a lot of healing into my heart and uncovered some of the roots of my fear. Fear no longer has a grip on my life.

But because of the fear I've experienced, I understand its power to keep us shackled to what's comfortable and known. Fear makes me withdraw, put up walls, and hunker down until the danger has passed. However, God's calling on our lives, and His best for us, are seldom found in safe zones.

To truly uncover our potential and become the women God sees in us, we must address fear. We must face what scares us and learn to overcome what debilitates us.

Much of what remains undone in our lives can be traced back to fear of some kind. And fear can be a tricky emotion to understand. That's partly due to different types of fear, some healthy and others unhealthy.

Healthy versus Unhealthy Fear

Healthy fears keep us safe and give us a respectful relationship with potentially hurtful things. A child learns not to touch a hot stove, and the fear of being burned keeps the child safe. As adults we learn that driving too fast is dangerous and expensive, and the fear of hurting others and our pocketbook reminds us to be safe on the road. We learn that certain people are unsafe, and we stay away from them.

The Bible talks of the fear of God as being a good thing. This is not a fear that drives us from God but rather allows us to approach Him with a healthy awe and respect. "In the fear of the LORD one has strong confidence, and his children will have a refuge" (Prov. 14:26 ESV). When we have this type of healthy respect for God, we actually make better decisions. "The fear of the LORD is the beginning of knowledge, but fools despise wisdom and instruction" (1:7).

We need healthy fear in our lives. We need to understand the connection between our choices today and the consequences of tomorrow. Perhaps if we made stronger connections between the two we would make different decisions. It's too easy to ignore consequences when they aren't immediate and think, *That won't happen to me*. With a healthy fear of consequences and of God, we can make good choices and avoid procrastination.

Conversely, there are fears that aren't good for us. These fears keep us from living out God's call on our lives, pursuing our dreams, or speaking our minds. Examples of these fears include facing the truth about ourselves, the opinions of others, failure, success, losing control, and being rejected.

The experiences of our past can cause a fear response that influences how we react to today's challenges. We've all had some pain in our past, and these wounds, even while in a stage of healing, can cause us to take a defensive posture, protecting ourselves from further pain.

Sometimes it's hard to tell the difference between a healthy fear and an unhealthy one, especially when our hearts feel shaky. So here's a simple guideline: healthy fears drive us to make good decisions, while unhealthy fears do the opposite.

Now let's weave that understanding into our procrastination discussion. Since we've already defined procrastination as an intentional delay of something that it is in our best interest to do, then unhealthy fear becomes a contributing factor.

Let's say Claire is an up-and-coming marketing executive but fears she doesn't have what it takes to succeed. She's afraid to push herself professionally, because what if she *proves* she doesn't have what it takes? Then she might discover that her college major and career choice were mistakes, thereby disappointing her parents and herself. So rather than press into the work and test her skills, she procrastinates. However, she blames it on her overloaded schedule.

Sophia is a mom who fears she'll never measure up to the other moms in her son's playgroup. They seem to have Pinterest-perfect lives while her home is a mess. Feeling like her efforts will never match the expectations of others, she puts off clearing the clutter and cleaning her home. Rather than being honest about her reasons, she makes offhand derogatory comments about moms who'd rather spend time cleaning than with their children.

Both women's fear causes them to shy away from work that would make a positive impact in their lives. Both women also fail to see fear as the source of their resistance to do that work.

Fear Is Woven in Tight

Fear is one of the biggest reasons we procrastinate. The problem is it's woven so deeply into our hearts that it's hard to identify. We've gotten so good at creating isolated lives, avoiding certain people or situations, and making excuses that we don't know how to deal with our fear. So when it pops up, rather than face it we make changes to avoid it.

We put off the phone call, the project, or the discussion, hoping the problem will resolve itself or we'll feel stronger and better able to face it tomorrow. Then we step back into our safe little bubble for a while until we have to step out and delay yet again.

Fear is hard to deal with, there's no doubt. Not only is its grip on us strong, but it appears fast and furiously, and sometimes with no warning. Burka and Yuen describe it this way: "Fear is triggered so rapidly, it's incredible. If you touch your arm, it takes your brain 400–500 milliseconds to register the sensation. But fear is registered in a mere 14 milliseconds."[1]

We're conditioned to react so quickly to fear that we don't even acknowledge it as fear. A sight, smell, or sound can trigger it and we're already changing course before we know it.

If left unaddressed, unhealthy fear causes us to slam on the brakes when we should be pressing the gas. It causes us to play it safe when we should be stepping out in faith. And it causes us to delay doing whatever we think might cause us fear.

Oh, do I understand this. If you listed every emotion humans experience in order from worst to best, fear would be at the top of my list. Fear makes me feel helpless and victimized. And as a woman who likes to be in control, I'll do just about anything to avoid feeling fear.

This is a lesson God continues to teach me over and over again. My whole life has been consumed with playing it safe, and while I'm not going to brag that I'm jumping out of airplanes now, I can tell you that God has done some major work in my heart when it comes to fear.

And I don't think I'm alone. So many of us intentionally avoid situations where we know we'll be afraid, causing us to create safe lives where we aren't tested or pushed out of our comfort zones.

Maybe you've procrastinated on things you believe will cause fear. It could be public speaking or facing a medical test. Maybe it's addressing someone who has wronged you or asking for a raise. Maybe it's changing careers or churches but you fear what your friends will say.

I'm convinced this is not God's plan. He doesn't want us to live our lives making choices in order to avoid fear. In fact, God doesn't want us to be afraid at all. He wants our trust in Him to be so complete that we will walk into the unknown with confidence.

However, God also knows us. He knows fear is a big part of our lives. That's why He's addressed it many times in His Word.

God Knows We Are Afraid

I've taught quite a bit at my home church, and one time I was asked in an event-planning meeting if I get nervous before I speak.

I answered, "No, I'm not nervous here." I was thinking about that setting, with these women whom I knew and loved.

Another woman responded by saying, "That's how you can tell you are in God's will, if you don't have any fear."

I didn't want to correct her in front of people, or tell her how much I've actually been afraid at other speaking events, but I couldn't disagree more. I had felt fear when speaking, and I probably would again.

God's people have always felt fear. In the Bible, there are almost two hundred references to people being afraid. The New Revised Standard version has sixty-six verses where the exact words "do not be afraid" are used. Here are some examples:

God told Abraham, "Do not be afraid."
God told Isaac, "Do not be afraid."
God told Jacob, "Do not be afraid."
God told Moses, "Do not be afraid."
God told Joshua, "Do not be afraid."

I could go on. Why do you think God had to tell the heroes of our faith not to be afraid? It's because they *were* afraid! They weren't feeling confident, strong, or courageous. They were feeling fear.

Here's the truth about those mighty men and women, hand-picked by God to carry out bold adventures and who saw God perform miracles: they didn't let fear stop them! They took the first step of obedience in the midst of their fears.

The Bible also includes examples of times when fear did stop the people of God from being obedient. One of them is probably the most famous story in the Old Testament—when the Israelites escape from captivity.

God gave a surprising response when His people were afraid. It's not what I would have expected, but it gives me a picture of

God's true heart toward dealing with fear, especially when that fear stops us from doing the right thing.

Exodus 14 tells of the Israelites' escape from Pharaoh, and the pursuit by the Egyptian army. The Israelites dead-ended at the edge of the Red Sea. With impassable water in front of them and over six hundred chariots on their heels, they were terrified. The people cried out to God and complained to Moses. They were so afraid they expressed a desire to be back in slavery in Egypt.

> As Pharaoh approached, the Israelites looked up, and there were the Egyptians, marching after them. They were terrified and cried out to the LORD. They said to Moses, "Was it because there were no graves in Egypt that you brought us to the desert to die? What have you done to us by bringing us out of Egypt? Didn't we say to you in Egypt, 'Leave us alone; let us serve the Egyptians'? It would have been better for us to serve the Egyptians than to die in the desert!" (Exod. 14:10–12)

Moses, a gentle and compassionate leader, reminded the people of God's faithfulness.

> Moses answered the people, "Do not be afraid. Stand firm and you will see the deliverance the LORD will bring you today. The Egyptians you see today you will never see again. The LORD will fight for you; you need only to be still." (vv. 13–14)

Moses is like a kind grandfather in this situation, filled with faith. And on the surface, there seems nothing wrong with Moses's encouragement. But God's answer in this particular situation is a bit different. Rather than telling the Israelites to stand still, He propels them to action.

> Then the LORD said to Moses, "Why are you crying out to me? Tell the Israelites to *move on*." (v. 15, emphasis added)

God knows where He's taking His people. He knows it's a beautiful land where they will live free. And God also knows these people have just recently seen Him perform some crazy miracles to set them free. And they stand there complaining, frozen in fear and resigned to die.

Why did they stop trusting Him? After how far God had brought them, why would they doubt Him?

Isn't that just like us? Fear causes us to freeze, to go another way, to avoid the problem. But when our fear is keeping us from moving toward God's best for our lives, we've *got to move*. We've got to choose to trust God—and do it afraid.

We Can Learn to Deal with Fear

When fear stops us from doing the right and best things in our lives, it's time to address it. I know this isn't an easy topic. But the only way to deal with fear is to call it out where it can't hide or control us anymore.

As I mentioned, I know what it's like to live with controlling fear. I could write an entire book on the subject. As God has brought healing to my heart over the years, I've learned there are two main roots of fear in my life. And these two fears, when unaddressed, can affect all the decisions I make, including my decision to procrastinate.

These two sources of fear are misplaced trust and misplaced identity.

Misplaced Trust

One of the challenges of being a Christian is learning to trust God. After all, how can we trust Someone we don't see? It's much easier to believe in God much like we believe the facts in a history book. A faith based on head knowledge is "safe" because it doesn't call us outside our comfortable, known world.

But that's not the life we are called to when we accept Jesus as Lord and submit our lives to Him. God asks us to do more than believe *in* Him. He asks us to *believe* Him. Believe Him when He says He is an ever-present source of help. Believe that He will never leave us or forsake us.

God is completely trustworthy, but we prefer to trust in ourselves, our job, our bank account, and so on.

But deep in our hearts, we know security isn't found in temporal things. We know we're undependable. We know others will let us down. We know the economy can tank. We know our health can change. So we live in this fearful world, not trusting God and not trusting ourselves.

When I put my trust in something other than God, my confidence is shaky, and fear has an open door.

- I doubt whether I can handle doing the work and fear the demands of success if I do manage to pull it off.
- I procrastinate as a way to control my future because I fear losing control more than the pain of procrastination.
- I delay obeying God's call to a new career because I fear the unknown.
- I put off scheduling doctor's appointments because I fear the results.

When our trust is rightly placed in God, we know that whatever our future holds, we are held by the hands of a loving God.

This idea of misplaced trust was central to God freeing me from a fear that led me straight into disobedient procrastination. After 9/11, I became increasingly afraid of flying until I flat-out refused to do it. In fact, my fear increased just when I had started to speak publicly.

So I stopped speaking anywhere I had to travel by plane. It wasn't the best career move, but I didn't care. I wasn't getting on an airplane.

It got worse, until I didn't even want to drive by the airport. My fear was irrational, and no amount of logic helped me work through it. No statistics from my husband or assurances from my friends helped.

The worst part was I never told anyone how deeply afraid I was. It was embarrassing to admit, especially since I was a leader in women's ministry and supposedly a strong Christian. When I did mention it, I sort of laughed it off, hoping it would seem normal. But it wasn't normal and it wasn't healthy.

I'd love to tell you the whole story, but by learning to pray against spiritual attack, I was miraculously freed from that fear by God. In the process, a truth about my faith was uncovered. I realized it was much easier to say I trusted God with my life than to *actually* trust Him. Fear got a grip on my heart because I had misplaced my trust.

Saying we trust God and actually trusting Him are two very different things.

Rather than trusting God to keep me safe, I trusted the pilot, the weather, the plane's engines, the air traffic controllers, and the mechanics who did the precheck. But deep in my heart I knew I couldn't trust them with my life. So fear crept in and took over. Satan saw that fear as a foothold to get me to be disobedient. And it worked. I delayed answering God's call to speak because of that fear.

When I acknowledged that fear and misplaced trust, I first confessed it to God. Then I started declaring my trust in God even though I didn't *feel* it. And I now fly completely free from fear.

Misplaced Identity

When our identity is based on results, we will avoid any risk of undesirable outcomes. Basically, we feel it's safer to do nothing than to risk and fail. If we fail, that means we are a failure.

Why do we draw a straight line from our actions to our identity? We are so quick to connect dots that aren't there, slap a label on ourselves, and believe it to be true. We stumble and call ourselves clumsy. We forget to pay a bill and call ourselves stupid. Our home is cluttered and we call ourselves pathetic.

Those aren't lines God draws. Only Satan draws a line from our work to our worth. Only our enemy wants us to find our identity in what we do, because he knows when the work is gone so is our sense of value.

God, however, has another identity for us, one that's unchanging and independent of our actions. It's as His chosen and beloved child. John 1:12 says, "Yet to all who did receive him, to those who believed in his name, he gave the right to become children of God."

When we are confident in our position as a child of God, we trust He will act on our behalf. Luke 18:7 says, "And will not God bring about justice for his chosen ones, who cry out to him day and night? Will he keep putting them off?"

Our identity is *not* defined by our actions, and so we will never be a "failure" when our performance doesn't match our expectations. When we reassign the source of our value and worth to its rightful place, we will be free from the fear of failure or of the opinions of others.

The only thing that matters is what our heavenly Father thinks about us. We can rest knowing we are safe and secure in God's unconditional love.

Let's Redefine "Failure"

I wish we could rewind our lives like the old VCR tapes and go back to the time when we learned that a mistake or a disappointing result equaled failure. Maybe it goes back to being afraid of a red

F on a test—or worse, on a report card. Maybe you grew up in an environment where nothing you did was good enough. Whatever the reason, many of us live in fear of failing, so much so that we live very insulated lives.

What could we do if we removed that fear of failing? What if we never doubted our value and knew, in the deepest places of our hearts, that our identity was unshakable?

I think we'd rush to do challenging work rather than postpone it. We'd be like children, excited to try something new. Anxious to test our strengths.

I've never seen a child afraid to learn to walk. No! They toddle, fall, laugh, and get back up. They know they don't know how to walk, but they're willing to fall multiple times in order to learn.

Thomas Edison "failed" thousands of times while he was practicing on the lightbulb. When people suggested he quit, his reply was, "I have gotten lots of results! If I find 10,000 ways something won't work, I haven't failed. I am not discouraged, because every wrong attempt discarded is often a step forward."[2]

The only true failure is to never try.

Understanding Our Fears

Fear isn't the reason behind every procrastination. But it's often there. It might be buried deep, protected by avoidance and defensiveness. In order to be free of fear, we must uncover it. We must face it and remove its power with the truth of God's protection over us and our identity in Him.

Take some time to peel back the layers on some of your choices and see if fear is a reason behind them. If so, you can go forward in confidence, knowing God will not fail you.

A Psalm for Fear

When my youngest son was little, he had nightmares. And every night we prayed against those nightmares and read Psalm 91. But I didn't just read it, I inserted his name where there was a pronoun. Years later, when God was freeing me from my fear of flying, He prompted me to read that same psalm. Only this time, my name was inserted. Here are a few verses with my name:

> "Because [Glynnis] loves me," says the LORD, "I will rescue [her]; I will protect [her], for [she] acknowledges my name. [Glynnis] will call on me, and I will answer [her]; I will be with [Glynnis] in trouble, I will deliver [her] and honor [her]. With long life I will satisfy [Glynnis] and show [her] my salvation." (Ps. 91:14–16)

Try this for yourself. Write it out on a 3x5 card and tuck it in your purse. Then when fear whispers *stop*, you can respond with the truth and press into obedience and your best work.

● PRACTICAL APPLICATION

Could fear be a reason for not addressing your daily task and your bigger goal? Let's say you've picked "opening and dealing with mail" as the task you want to address. What is there to fear about opening mail? Well, perhaps you are tight on finances and it's hard to see a bill when you know you are going to be late in paying it again. That would definitely cause you to stack up each day's batch until you felt strong enough to deal with it. Perhaps that fear is rooted in a misplaced trust of who is truly your provider.

Spend a few minutes praying about your personal goals. Ask God to reveal any fear that might be hidden. Then write the answer.

My regular task:

My personal goal:

7

Too Busy?

I sat on my couch with tears dripping. No amount of "get yourself together" talk could stop the flow. Tissue after wadded tissue piled on the coffee table in front of me. Nothing tragic had happened, but I just couldn't stop crying.

It seemed like everybody wanted or needed something from me. Demands lined up like ants carrying crumbs, an endless, constant stream. No matter how hard or fast I worked, I couldn't keep up. Early mornings and late nights bookended exhausted, caffeine-filled days. It felt like I was scooping water out of a swimming pool with a teaspoon. Hopeless.

That day in my living room, my inadequacies loomed large. *Why did I think I could manage a new volunteer position? Why did my hand go up in that meeting? Why did I say yes to so many things that now feel like burdens about to sink me?*

I felt like such a fraud, acting like I could manage such a heavy workload. But I didn't want anyone to know I was beyond my capacity to manage all my responsibilities.

So rather than face the fact that I had too much on my plate, I soldiered on, with procrastination as my coping mechanism to avoid the truth. But the truth caught up with me that day on the couch. I was too busy.

There was too much to do and too little of me to do it. Whenever this happened, I would deal with the problem that screamed loudest. Kind of like a whack-a-mole game, where you respond out of instinct. And so each day I shifted my priorities based on which deadline was most pressing, which emergency was most dire, and who was yelling the loudest.

Sadly, when I get too busy, I just react. Not always wisely or kindly. And when I do not press the pause button to reevaluate, I'm just a walking disaster.

150 Percent Doesn't Fit in 100 Percent

The problem for me is I live on this invisible line between a manageable schedule and being too busy. And I know I'm not alone. Ask a friend how she's doing, and the answer will likely be "busy" or "tired" or both.

Too many of us are trying to fit too many activities and responsibilities into our lives without having the capacity to manage it all. We end up working from the moment we get up till the moment we collapse into bed. But even then our minds are still going, robbing us of the sleep we need to get up the next day and do it all again.

We're simply trying to do too much. Much more than we were ever designed to do. And, I'd like to suggest, more than we need to do. Our expectations about our time and energy are simply unrealistic. We're like Cinderella's stepsisters trying to squeeze our feet into that glass slipper.

A few years ago, my two daughters and I were doing some baking and I watched my life being put on display with a measuring cup.

Flour-dusted shirts, sticky hands, and happy faces gathered in my kitchen as an afternoon of baking unfolded. The counters were covered with bowls, spoons, and ingredients as my young daughters eagerly helped with the culinary creation we were assembling.

Part of the learning process that day involved reading the recipe and getting out ingredients and utensils. So when the recipe called for 1½ cups of milk, I directed one girl to get the two-cup measuring cup from the cabinet. She made it to the right cabinet, but picked out the one-cup measure instead.

Instead of correcting her, I showed my daughters how to make that size work. We filled up the measuring cup once, then filled it to half the second time. Then I showed them the two-cup measure and explained how it was big enough to hold all the milk the recipe required.

Then I got creative and decided to throw in some math. I explained how we couldn't put twelve ounces of liquid into an eight-ounce container. The excitement of the "lesson" took hold, and I jumped into percentages, saying you can't put 150 percent of something into 100 percent.

Their glazed looks told me I should have stopped a few minutes earlier.

Days later, I realized that teachable moment during baking was meant for me as much as for them. As I thought about this principle of measurement, I realized it doesn't work with milk and it doesn't work in life. Yet so many of us try to cram twelve hours of work into eight, and eight hours of work into four.

And then we wonder why we can't find a healthy balance in life. We'll never find peace when the demands on our time and energy exceed our capacity. We will end up procrastinating on something. And usually that something will have the biggest impact on our highest goals. Being overbusy reduces us to maintenance mode rather than growth mode.

Overload Is a Heart Condition

As I pondered the question of why so many women I know are living overloaded lives, I came upon a common theme: we want something we don't have. Here are some of the desires that cause us to jam-pack our schedules:

We don't want to miss an opportunity.
We don't want our children to miss out on their potential.
We don't want to be left out.
We want to feel needed.
We want to feel important.
We want to be respected.
We want more things.
We don't know how to have fun or relax so we stay busy.

Each of these reasons reveals an unmet need in our hearts. It's always there. We might believe we're victims of circumstances, but very few people are. Author Tim Kreider presents the idea that we are overbusy by choice:

> It isn't generally people pulling back-to-back shifts in the I.C.U. or commuting by bus to three minimum-wage jobs who tell you how busy they are; what those people are is not busy but *tired*. *Exhausted. Dead on their feet*. It's almost always people whose lamented busyness is purely self-imposed: work and obligations they've taken on voluntarily, classes and activities they've "encouraged" their kids to participate in. They're busy because of their own ambition or drive or anxiety, because they're addicted to busyness and dread what they might have to face in its absence.[1]

I think he's right. There is an unmet need in my heart that drives me to take on more than I can manage—a discontent that pushes me to pack my schedule. And when there is no margin in my schedule, my life is a rush. Overload and hurry always hold hands.

I remember when it started for me. It was when God answered the prayers of my heart for children. I was overjoyed to start our family with three healthy boys (God added our daughters ten years later), but the plan was for them not to change my life too much. I was so deceived.

So when they were young, you would have found me rushing from one task to another, usually pushing or dragging a frustrated child. I was either in high gear or crashing in the aftermath of the frenzy . . . often holding back tears and berating myself for not being able to get it together.

It was an exhausting way to live. But an inner drive to achieve fueled the fury of my days. Refusing to admit I couldn't do it all, I tried to keep up my same pre-child schedule. But of course, God had added three little boys to my responsibilities.

Sadly, everyone in my family paid the price, especially my little guys, who weren't genetically wired to sit quietly and color while Mommy attended a meeting.

During that time, "Hurry up or we'll be late" was commonly heard, either yelled from the kitchen or hissed while we scurried into the back row at church. There was too much to do in too little time. Life was a blur.

And I thought everyone lived like this. That was until I read about "hurry sickness" in *The Life You've Always Wanted* by John Ortberg. My heart was skewered when I read that one of its symptoms is a diminished capacity to love. My children could have told you I had a problem. Only it wasn't hurry sickness, it was hurry *addiction*.

God dealt with my addiction to overload and hurry by taking it all away in a cross-country move. He made me go cold turkey as I said goodbye to working at my job, directing the children's ministry, coleading the women's ministry, being on the praise team, having my small group, leading Vacation Bible Study each summer, and more.

God moved us 2,100 miles away—so far that I couldn't even sneak back to lead a women's event.

I had no job, no church, and no friends, just lots of time. Since two of the boys were in school and the youngest had just started preschool, I had plenty of time to think and pray. And while there were lots of tears, I also experienced God in a new way.

Very quickly, God connected me with Proverbs 31 Ministries. I started to learn that God had a better plan for my life than I did, and that I should look to Him for direction on my daily activities. I also learned that my first line of ministry was inside my home.

I wasn't completely cured of my hurry addiction yet, so I decided I would become the Best Homemaker Ever. And then I picked up a book called *No Ordinary Home* by Carol Brazo. And right in the beginning of the book I read something that brought about the biggest change in my life:

> If there were one biblical truth I wish I could give my children and lay hold of in my own deepest parts, it would be this one thing. He created me, He loves me, He will always love me. Nothing I do will change who I am.
>
> Being versus doing. The error was finally outlined in bold. I was always worried about what I was doing. . . . God's only concern was and is what I am being—a child of His, forgiven, justified by the work of His Son, His Heir.[2]

You know when you feel like an author has peeked into your living room window and knows exactly who you are? That's what reading this was like for me.

God wired me to be highly productive, but I hadn't undergirded that with an understanding of my true identity. So in order to feel worthwhile and valued and confident, I was driven to take on more. More accomplishments equaled more worth.

But it was never enough.

Someone once asked multimillionaire John D. Rockefeller, "How much money is enough?" He answered, "Just a little bit more."[3]

For women who have placed our worth in our work, we're certain just a little bit more to do will fill the hole in our hearts. But it won't, and we end up feeling rushed, overwhelmed, and filled with regret.

I didn't want to be that woman who rushed through life. I didn't want my children to look back and say, "Wow, Mom got a lot done!" I wanted them to be convinced, thoroughly and utterly, of my love for them. And not just my children, but my husband, parents, sisters, and so on.

That was when I started to seriously address my issue of being too busy. And I realized I had the potential to overload my schedule whether I was unemployed, employed outside the home, or working from home (which I do now). The circumstances of my life didn't make it easier or harder for me to work less. The issue was inside me.

The truth is, a homeschooling mom can be busier than an executive. And a retired person can be more hurried than a working mom of five. Overload is a condition of our hearts. It's the result of following our own to-do list rather than God's.

Not everyone reading this book is too busy. But if you use "too busy" as a reason for your procrastination, then take some time to think through your motivation for overloading yourself. It will look different from mine. Your heart is seeking something that only God can provide.

Once you've identified your motivation, you are ready to start dealing with the practical steps of reducing the amount of activities, work, and responsibilities that fill your calendar. The challenge will be to assess what's most important to you, then edit out the rest.

Identifying Our Priorities

If you've ever been in that crazy-busy place, you know the most urgent issues, the ones that fill your day, aren't always the most important ones. And if you've become chronically chaotic, you might not even know what your priorities are anymore.

That's because the most important needs in our life tend to be the quiet ones. Of course, when we have children, they are both important and loud. But even with our children we can procrastinate by addressing their most urgent needs and postponing the quiet ones.

When our schedules are overloaded, we push the hushed, undemanding needs to the bottom of our lists. The ones that don't shout for attention are the ones we plan on addressing tomorrow. Or the next day, when things settle down. However, when we tend toward overload, tomorrow is just as busy.

I don't know what your quiet priorities are, but those that get pushed to the bottom of my list include time with my mother and sisters, exercise, studying the Bible, and having fun, to name just a few. The dreams of my heart speak in a whisper, not a roar. Especially when I press them down over and over. With my children, one quiet priority is time without an agenda, so our conversation can naturally flow.

These priorities don't shout at me; they just patiently wait for my attention. German poet Johann Wolfgang von Goethe said, "Things that matter most must never be at the mercy of things that matter least."[4]

If you find yourself in a place of not knowing what is important, consider asking God. The Bible tells us God freely gives us wisdom, and that's what we need most.

In James 1:5–8, we find instructions on how to ask God for wisdom. We can't just say "God, tell me what to do," and stop there. This passage gives us a condition for receiving wisdom, and that's to believe God will give it.

> If any of you lacks wisdom, you should ask God, who gives generously to all without finding fault, and it will be given to you. But when you ask, you must believe and not doubt, because the one who doubts is like a wave of the sea, blown and tossed by the wind. That person should not expect to receive anything from the Lord. Such a person is double-minded and unstable in all they do.

How can you be sure it's God answering and not your own thoughts? I've discovered it's a process. First, we can be sure God will never tell us anything against His Word. So if you ask God if you should resign from the PTA, and you believe God is telling you not to resign but instead to steal the money from the cash box so you can buy your family dinner on meeting nights, well, you can be positive that message is not from Him.

So ask God for wisdom to know what to do. And when you get an idea, even if it's a feeling, and it doesn't contradict God's Word and it's in line with His character, then trust that God is giving you direction. Each time you ask and don't doubt, you'll feel more confident you are hearing from God.

Is Busy Really That Bad?

Even though this chapter is about being too busy, I want to make sure to clarify that busy isn't bad. In fact, the Bible actually encourages us to be busy and productive.

> Likewise, teach the older women to be reverent in the way they live, not to be slanderers or addicted to much wine, but to teach

what is good. Then they can urge the younger women to love their husbands and children, to be self controlled and pure, to be busy at home, to be kind, and to be subject to their husbands, so that no one will malign the word of God. (Titus 2:3–5)

I also love this verse: "We hear that some among you are idle and disruptive. They are not busy; they are busybodies" (2 Thess. 3:11).

Being busy isn't the problem. The problem is being a *busybody*—or getting involved in things that don't concern us. When we take on responsibilities that aren't ours to assume, we are ineffective in what we *are* called to do and consequently lead lives that are filled to overflowing.

What the Bible *doesn't* say is that we need to be busy all the time. This is where we need wisdom to know when to work and when to stop. We need to build margins into our days so that we can enjoy life. God gave us the Sabbath to make sure we'd stop working one day a week, but it's a common commandment to break, as we use it as a catch-up day for our work.

To manage our schedules well, we need to know our capacity and not accept more responsibility than we can manage.

But we can't start to design a manageable schedule until we do a personal inventory of all we have to get done. This is painful, I will warn you. But finding out the truth will set you free from the bondage of being too busy.

Taking a Personal Inventory

As God took me on a journey toward having a healthy schedule, my first task was to take a personal inventory. I had to write down everything I had to do on one piece of paper . . . which turned into two.

I included phone calls to make, emails to send, projects to start, and other projects to finish. The list included things I needed to do that day and things I needed to do that month. It included ongoing responsibilities like grocery shopping and one-time events like coordinating the T-shirt sales at my children's school.

I kept that paper on the counter because I continued to think of things to add—for days. Things I *meant* to do but had abandoned. Things I *had* to do but had forgotten. Dreams I'd given up on.

It was painful and overwhelming. But it was also a relief. Once all my responsibilities were in one place, my problem was obvious. I was trying to fit 150 percent into 100 percent of my life. It would never fit.

My life had to be simplified, which meant reducing the demands on my time. Some things were easy to cut; I'd been holding on to them for too long anyway. Others took longer, as I had to fulfill a commitment. As a family, we decided to make some changes to our children's activities. I stopped doing everything for my children and trained them to take on some household jobs.

A year of editing that list resulted in a manageable, more focused, and more productive life. I also learned a new way to manage my work, but I'll tell you more about that in chapter 13.

It was a year of hard decisions, but it was worth the peace I gained.

That year I learned I have exactly enough time to do what God wants me to do. No more. Ecclesiastes 3:1 says, "There is a time for everything, and a season for every activity under the heavens." My key to balance is seeking God's will for me in my current season and not spending time on assignments meant for other people.

Earlier, I mentioned my addiction to hurry, and while I don't think "hurry addiction" will enter the books as a true psychological condition, I constantly deal with my struggle to overcommit. And even with my best intentions, I can find myself being too busy.

When I'm there, I do a heart check and discover where I've gotten off track. I do a schedule check and start editing. With God's wisdom and an updated master list of all my commitments, I get ongoing reality checks. And although I'm not really good at math, I do remember that 150 percent of something will never fit in a 100 percent container.

● PRACTICAL APPLICATION

What does your "perfect" schedule look like? Take some time to write down what you wish you had time for. This list *shouldn't* include things like washing the dishes. But it should include things like having fun with your children or regular date nights with your husband. Save this list and schedule time for one of these "shoulds" in the next week. You'll feel empowered to master your time rather than being mastered by it.

Now let's return to your two personal objectives and consider how your time will be affected as you begin to better manage these two areas of your life. When you develop good habits on your everyday task and start working toward your bigger goal, how will that positively affect your time or schedule?

My regular task:

My personal goal:

8

Thinking with Focus and Clarity

Some days my problem is I just can't think clearly.

Too many things battle for my attention. My thoughts feel scattered and I can't focus enough to tackle anything of value. At the end of a day like that, it seems I didn't accomplish anything. I worked nonstop but have nothing to show for it except maybe a few less emails.

Working hard isn't the problem. I can push my body to get things done. But working effectively, tackling important projects . . . that takes focus.

We take our ability to think clearly for granted. However, in our too-busy, information-laden society, clarity of thought is getting harder to come by. We live with a poverty of attention that infiltrates and sabotages our focus, and ultimately, our work.

Mental focus is an important tool in a procrastinator's toolbox. Without the ability to assess and prioritize our multitude of tasks, we'll just pick the one that requires the least amount of focus. And usually that's not what we should be doing first.

Hence the important projects, the life-giving ones, the game-changers, they get pushed back until . . . well, until we feel like we can concentrate. Only those moments don't come often enough and we start down the path of procrastination once again.

Unfortunately, we take our minds for granted. We assume we are always thinking at our best, but that's not the case. We need to treat our minds much like a chef treats knives. With care.

Every chef knows a sharp knife is safer and more efficient. Have you ever tried dicing a tomato with a dull knife? You get mush.

But a sharp knife allows for finer, quicker, smarter work. That's how we should approach our thinking. When we think more clearly, we'll be able to prioritize our work, and subsequently work more productively.

The good news is we can sharpen our focus. And for most of us it doesn't take a prescription. Simple adaptations in our daily routines will make a difference.

There are several common reasons why we can feel fuzzy and unable to address more complicated tasks. Before we get into these, let's start with understanding and working with our design as humans. Too often we overestimate our capacity and underestimate the care needed to maintain the body and brain God gave us. Then we'll address some societal changes that have snuck in and watered down our attention. I'm convinced our ability to problem-solve will eliminate a good portion of our procrastination issues.

We're Only Human

We are the gatekeepers of our bodies and minds; how we treat ourselves matters. Yet technology has introduced a dangerous expectation into our beliefs: we should be able to operate at our best at all times.

At any given moment, I want to be able to apply my mind fully, with accuracy and creativity, to whatever task is put before me. I push myself to achieve that goal, expecting my mind to obey my commands.

However, we weren't designed to operate like a computer—at full speed, continuously, for long periods of time. Processing data in milliseconds and without error.

Oh, how I wish I could. And I'm quite impatient when I face my human limitations. When I find myself mentally sluggish, have trouble making decisions, or feel like I've hit a brick wall, I get annoyed and frustrated with myself.

How unfair of me to expect that of myself! I'm not a machine. I'm a human created by a loving God with intricacy and intentionality. And with a need to rest, both physically and mentally.

The more I honor the design of the Creator, the more effective I am in my ability to prioritize, manage, and complete the daily tasks and big goals that God has assigned me.

Let's look at sleep, for example. I used to wonder why God designed us to need sleep. What motivated Him to factor into our design a requirement that our bodies shut down for seven to eight hours of sleep a day? I know there are restorative processes happening when we sleep, but couldn't God have made that happen while we eat?

Doesn't making us need sleep seem so inefficient? Why not design us to go, go, go? I could get so much more done without sleep.

And yet, the more I learn about God, the more I understand we were created for so much more than mere productivity. We were created for relationship. Dependent relationships, in fact. First with Him, then with others.

As I come to understand and accept I was created with what on the surface seem like weaknesses, two things happen. First, unhealthy pride is eliminated. It's hard to be prideful when I realize how vulnerable I really am. I'm not invincible. I can't work nonstop Second, I find myself depending more upon God for strength. My independent nature still struggles with this, but I'm convinced God delights in my need for Him.

So while science can never prove *those* two reasons for the necessity of sleep, I've accepted them as a fact of life.

Many of us want to find the magic bullet for time management or productivity. I've certainly read my share of books on those subjects. *What tricks will help me get it all done? What app will make me more efficient?*

Certainly we can all use the wisdom of others who are learning to be more productive, given the challenges of today. But the more we understand the purpose in our physical needs, and honor them through healthy choices, the better able we are to discover real, sustainable productivity.

Charge and Recharge

Humans are designed to work in cycles. We expend energy and then recharge. In fact, scientists have learned we process through 90- to 120-minute cycles throughout the day called the ultradian rhythm.

Most of us know such a rhythm exists in sleep, when we move through four stages of non-REM (Rapid Eye Movement) into REM sleep. But it also happens during waking hours.

Imagine this rhythm much like an auto-shutoff mechanism that protects an electronic device from overheating. Our minds self-protect by diminishing concentration about every ninety minutes and enforcing a mental break.

Rather than honoring this natural ebb and flow of attention and energy and giving ourselves a mental and physical rest, we push through by using artificial ways to recharge. Sometimes it's something sweet or starchy to eat, or something caffeinated—what I like to call a "liquid nap."

Rather than consume empty calories, we could employ a simple solution: stop working for ten to fifteen minutes and take a break. Not just for thirty seconds. We actually need to rest.

This will feel counterproductive, but it's not. In giving your mind and body a chance to recharge, you will actually return to your work with greater focus.

Imagine yourself as a Michelin-rated chef sharpening her knife. Here are some ideas for sharpening your mental blade:

- A ten-minute nap
- Playing with your child
- Listening to worship music
- Playing with a pet
- Taking a short walk
- Reading the Bible (try Psalms)
- Walking up and down stairs
- Watering plants
- Gardening
- Stretching
- Dancing to your favorite song

The Critical Importance of Sleep

We love to label our generations. There are the Boomers; the Busters; Gen X, Y, and Z. I'd like to propose a new one: the "E" generation. For exhaustion.

Is there anyone who isn't tired?

We've got a chronic sleep issue. In 2013, the US Centers for Disease Control and Prevention (CDC) called it a national health epidemic. In a Better Sleep Council survey, nearly eight in ten adults believe they need another hour of sleep to be more productive.[1]

The average adult needs seven to eight hours of sleep a night. Statistics vary, but a majority of us suffer from some amount of sleep deprivation. And the impact is profound, including increased health problems and accidents caused by drowsiness.

While science is still exploring and understanding what God designed, and we might not fully understand why, sleep is paramount to focus and good decision making. Without enough sleep, our ability to access higher-level cognitive functions is limited.

There are so many things to blame for our lack of sufficient sleep. There are the happy reasons, like a new baby or waiting up for a loved one to arrive at the airport.

Then there are the harder ones, like parenting teens with late curfews, sharing a bed with a snoring spouse, or owning a ninety-five-pound German Shepherd with incontinence problems that wakes you up at four in the morning because she wants you to open the back door rather than going out her doggy door. And believe me, when you have a ninety-five-pound four-legged girl who's a little leaky, you get up.

A good night's sleep is hard to get consistently. But the real problem is we accept it as a fact of life, something to suffer through in hopes of getting past this phase of sleeplessness and moving into a time of sweet dreams. Only that never happens. At least not for long. But if we want to operate at our optimum mental state, we must prioritize sleep.

My first experience with sleep deprivation was as a new mom. In fact, it hit me on day two of being a mother. I clearly remember having friends come by, pushing their nine-month-old in a stroller, and tears rolling down my face as I thought, *I bet they can sleep through the night.*

So if I felt like this on day two of motherhood, can you even imagine how I felt after that? I'd never been able to pull all-nighters in college or even stay up late, so when my wakefulness was enforced night after night with a crying baby I couldn't seem to help, I was a mess. I remember thinking, at two o'clock one morning while walking and rocking my crying Joshua, *This is why they use sleep deprivation as torture.*

• • • •

As I mentioned earlier, there was a time I resented sleep. Most likely because it's hard for me to function without it. But once I started learning about its God-designed value, I began to appreciate and value sleep like never before.

Critical things happen during sleep that don't happen during wakefulness. Researchers have learned that while we sleep, our brains catalog events that happened during the day, allowing us to form and consolidate memories we can use in the future.

One new exciting finding shows that the brain clears itself of "waste" when we sleep. This happens because the glymphatic system in the brain expands during sleep and allows the glial fluids to circulate, removing toxins.[2] This finding could have profound impact on understanding diseases like Alzheimer's. For us, it's one more reason to get enough sleep.

There are so many reasons why people don't sleep well that it would be simplistic and dishonoring to just tell you to sleep more. I know what it feels like to lie awake wide-eyed, body tired but mind refusing to shut off. And when we live with the burden of too much undone, it can be even worse.

As I've evaluated my own sleep issues, I've discovered a few practical habits that help me sleep better.

1. **Read my Bible before bed.** This is not the only time I read my Bible, but I find ending the day with God's truth to be the best way to center my mind on God's power and protection over me. This has helped me overcome worry that might keep me up.

2. **Do not schedule evening meetings.** For twenty years I've said no to any commitment requiring night meetings. I can handle them once in a while, but they make my mind race.

3. **Use white noise.** I incorporate this with a fan at home and with an app called Sleep Pillow when traveling. I also invested in sleep phones (think a soft headband with speakers) to cut out unusual noise.

4. **Define the lines between work and rest.** As a telecommuter, I could work around the clock. But I need a clear defining line between work and home life. So I've chosen to add something physical to my schedule to separate my work day from my evening. For example, I like to work out or take the dogs on a walk. This ends my work day and allows me enough time for my mind to rest.

5. **Do not use a computer screen at night.** Our bodies need dark to switch into sleep mode. Studies have shown that exposure to light limits the production of melatonin, which helps to regulate a good night's sleep. Some people take a melatonin supplement, but I prefer to try to limit the light. Which means my books are all made of old-fashioned paper.

Information Overload

Maybe the most insidious enemy of our ability to focus is information overload. The amount of information we filter each day is astounding. And with each fact, thought, or question, we have to sift and sort and find someplace to store it.

Daniel Levitin, author of *The Organized Mind*, says, "On a typical day, we take in the equivalent of about 174 newspapers' worth of information, five times as much as we did in 1986."[3]

Consider this statistic from former Google CEO Eric Schmidt: "There was 5 Exabytes of information created between the dawn of civilization through 2003, but that much information is now created every 2 days, and the pace is increasing."[4]

It's exhausting trying to sort through all that information and choose what to do with it all. Remember it? Save it? Share it? Trash it? We make so many infinitesimal decisions that we get what's called "information fatigue."

Have you ever felt that way trying to pick out a hairstyling product? I have no idea if I should choose mousse, gel, cream, crème (yes, these are two different products), balm, serum, custard, sculpting wax, pomade, or whip. Some of these sound like dessert options.

Simply put, we get analysis paralysis and feel like we can't make a good decision. Perhaps it's because we wonder if we have the right information we need. What if there is one more piece of information out there? That one perfect piece of data would enable us to make the perfect decision.

Another problem is we don't know who the "experts" are anymore. We used to know. They were our parents, teachers, and health care providers. Now we don't trust the experts anymore, and would rather look to our peers for advice even though we subliminally know they don't know much more than us.

Plus, who has time for all that research? And with all those thoughts brewing, I start to stress. This happens so quickly that I might not even notice it. But my brain does.

In fact, while I'm standing in the Target aisle looking at hair products, the lower part of my brain, the area related to survival response (the hypothalamus, hippocampus, and amygdala[5]), senses my frustration and releases neurotransmitters or stress hormones. Rather than *activating* my executive processing to help me make a decision, these chemicals actually *weaken* the influence of my prefrontal cortex.[6]

Most of us know this primitive response as the fight-or-flight response and understand its use when facing serious threats. What we are learning is it doesn't take much stress to activate this automatic response.

So rather than think logically and process a thoughtful response, we find our emotions taking over and we freeze up or respond in unwise ways—like abandoning ourselves to food or a mental escape.

Information overload creates serious problems for procrastinators, as we don't need any more excuses to abandon our best work. Remember that the definition of procrastination is a voluntary delay of something we could do but choose not to. We're experts at choosing alternatives to what we really need to do.

So how do we handle the onslaught of information coming our way?

As hard as it will be, we must go on an information diet and limit what we allow our minds to access. Here are some practical tips:

- Acknowledge you will not have all the information you need to make a perfect decision.
- Pray and seek God's direction when making a decision.
- Turn off push notifications.
- Stop watching the news.
- Read one book at a time. (All the book lovers gasp!)
- Cancel magazine subscriptions and delete email subscriptions.
- Schedule social media time into your day—don't switch over to it whenever you're bored.

Not only have you reduced the stream of information but you have also freed up time. Let's use it wisely.

Multitasking Is a Myth

Multitasking, another opponent of focus, is something we do all the time—and it's actually rewiring our brains in a way that makes it difficult for us to sustain focus when needed. In fact, we can lose up to 40 percent of our productivity when we multitask.[7]

We simply can't focus on two tasks at once. It takes .7 seconds for us to refocus every time we shift attention from one task to another. And some of us do this hundreds of times a day.

Here's what happens when we switch from task to task:

- It takes us longer to get things done.
- We make more mistakes.
- We have to refocus, which expends mental energy.
- We sacrifice creativity.

We've adopted a multitasking lifestyle in part to attempt to manage all the information we're presented with. So we switch from emails to texts to social media to the internet to an app and finally to the work we were supposed to be doing all along.

Mozilla Firefox, a web browser, reports the average user in my age group has three tabs open at one time.[8] Mercy! Once again, I'm above average in the worst sort of way. I usually have about eight tabs open. However, I'm proud to say I did shut down my emails in order to focus on writing. Though I did happen to watch a fun video . . . several times.

The solution to the cost of multitasking is very simple if we are willing to do it. We must retrain our brains by limiting input. This means turning things off and monotasking whenever possible.

I Have the Mind of Christ

First Corinthians 2:15–16 says, "The person with the Spirit makes judgments about all things, but such a person is not subject to merely human judgments, for, 'Who has known the mind of the Lord so as to instruct him?' But we have the mind of Christ."

This is good news for us. When we decide to follow Jesus as our Lord, God sends His Spirit to dwell in us. God's Spirit is available to help us think clearly and make decisions. This verse also tells us we have the "mind of Christ." But so often I ignore this divine help and try to solve problems in my natural thinking. Hence frustration, discouragement, and confusion. It's a downward spiral.

When I start to feel overwhelmed, the most productive thing I can do is to stop working and sit in God's presence. My natural mind might scream that it's a waste of time and I really should answer a few more emails or rewrite my to-do list instead. But when I quiet myself, and position myself to listen, then God's Spirit steps in with wisdom.

My reality may include cluttered and chaotic circumstances, but it also includes the Spirit of God and the mind of Christ. The natural mind hears the shouts of the urgent. The mind of Christ allows me to hear the whisper of God in the midst of it all.

Is the clutter in your mind making it hard to think clearly? Perhaps one of your problems is you're trying to figure things out on your own. You have been given the mind of Christ and you are offered the wisdom of God. So stop working, sit quietly, and allow God to cover your clouded thinking with His clarity.

● PRACTICAL APPLICATION

Consider your mental status at different times throughout the day. When are you sharpest? When do you feel weary? Are there times you feel foggy? By identifying your personal high and low points, you can strategize when to tackle your hardest and best work and when to work on easier tasks.

Now consider the two priorities you are addressing. In light of the new information you've learned in this chapter, when would be the best time to work on them? Do you need to minimize distractions or limit information? Do you need to practice monotasking?

What changes need to happen to better manage:

My regular task:

My personal goal:

9

Taming Our Perfectionist Instincts

I dread decorating at holidays. I put it off as long as possible, and usually only get to it when the guilt gets too uncomfortable and pushes me to do something. Well, perhaps I should clarify; it's not that I dislike home accessories. I actually love good design of every kind: graphics, home decor, and even cake decorating. I'm hooked on *Southern Living* magazine and HGTV. With all my heart, I want to be creative in some kind of design. But I seem to have little ability to bring things together into an attractive visual arrangement.

Years ago, I naively thought I was decent at decorating—until people started redoing my efforts. Whether at church or work, if I was assigned the setup of a table of any kind—snacks, desserts, book sales—someone would come along behind me and rearrange the items. It happened so often that I just stopped trying. I'd laugh it off and ask to be assigned something else.

Then I realized my home was boring compared to others. How did people find a screaming deal at a garage sale, buy some chalk paint and discount upholstery fabric, and turn an old dining room set into a magazine-worthy photo spread?

Ugh! It's hard to face a weakness. And because I so desperately want to be good at decorating, it hurts.

When I take a step back, I can see that my standard for decorating is ridiculous. I'm comparing my home, my income, my resources, and my style to others who are truly gifted in this area. Logically I should see that those comparisons and my personal expectations aren't fair, and give myself a break. I *should* enjoy decorating for the creative process it is and because I love it!

Only there's this critical voice inside me that says, *Admit defeat and give up*. In a quiet little hiss, it also says things like, *You'll never be happy with the results . . . someone will come along behind you and do it better . . . you aren't artistic . . . if you can't do it well, just forget it.*

That voice has a name: perfectionist. And it's not my friend.

One would think that the desire to do things well is an asset. And it is. But perfectionism isn't the pursuit of excellence. It's the pursuit of perfection. Excellence is possible is *some things*; perfection is possible in *nothing*. Excellence pushes us to *do* our best; perfectionism pushes us to *be* the best.

Perfectionism is the enemy of learning and growing and enjoying areas of life where we haven't achieved mastery. Which, if you're like me, are most areas of life. And we procrastinate addressing those areas for fear of feeling unsatisfied, critical, and discouraged.

How do we know when we're in an unhealthy pursuit of perfection? Here are a few questions to ask ourselves:

- Do I want to do things perfectly or not at all?
- Am I overly critical of myself?
- Am I overly critical of others?

- Do I see mistakes and possible pitfalls before others do?
- Do I always feel like I should be doing more?
- Does the thought of failing keep me from starting?
- Do I have trouble making decisions for fear of making the wrong one?
- Once I start a project, do I have trouble knowing when it's done?
- Do I feel like an imposter?

Does this sound like someone you know? Maybe even you? If so, it's possible you have some perfectionist tendencies.

Many procrastinators are also perfectionists. They have an unhealthy relationship with performance of any kind. It must be perfect or it must be nothing.

Never Good Enough

Perfectionism often starts in childhood, but not always in the same environment. Some perfectionists grew up with constant *disapproval*, never feeling good enough. Perhaps compared to a sibling, or to a parent's success, the child strives for approval that is always out of reach. Being "perfect" is the only acceptable way to get through life.

Others grew up with *conditional* love and approval. When the child performed to the standard of the parent, love was shown. And others grew up with an *emotionally distant* parent—not critical, not conditional acceptance, just neutral. "Daddy, look at me!" says the smiling little girl as she twirls in her Sunday best, hoping for some kind of approving word. She'll try harder and harder to get noticed through her performance, refining her work each time in hopes of finally earning a nod.

Since no one grew up with perfect parents, it makes sense that many of us struggle with perfectionism. And I haven't even mentioned the media images of perfect people with perfect lives! (Maybe not so much on reality TV, which has introduced us to a little too much reality.)

Perfectionist tendencies cause us to base our self-esteem on external approval, and we are left vulnerable and oversensitive to the opinions of others. We can lose perspective on what matters most and be internally driven to control situations and opinions of others through our work. Only we end up frustrated because we can't even meet our own expectations, much less the supposed expectations of others. And so perfectionists believe they'll never measure up and are highly self-condemning. Who needs enemies when we have such a brilliant inner critic?

However, we still dread criticism so much that we seek temporary relief in procrastination. Which leads to more self-criticism, leading to more procrastination, and so on.

Neil Fiore, PhD, in his book *The Now Habit*, describes the perfectionist cycle that leads to procrastination this way:

> As conflict builds between your internal fears of failure or imperfection and the external demands of others, you seek relief through procrastination. This can lead to a pernicious cycle: Perfectionistic demands lead to → fear of failure → PROCRASTINATION → self-criticism → anxiety and depression → loss of confidence → greater fear of failure which leads to → stronger need to use PROCRASTINATION as a temporary escape.[1]

What a hard cycle to break! Thankfully, with God's help we can identify and address this tendency before it consumes our lives. Let's take a deeper look at this issue and why it's got such a hold on us, starting with twelve years or more of training to meet external standards.

How School Didn't Help

Perfectionists loved their school days. It was there that we knew the rules and requirements and how to meet them. And being the teacher's pet was a side benefit.

For at least twelve years of our lives, we sat in classrooms where clear expectations were presented. We knew what chapters to read, what rubric to follow, and how to write a report the teacher would love. We knew that to earn an A, that gold star confirming our achievement, we had to produce excellent work.

Expectations were clearly defined in school. But in real life, that A is elusive. And there's no one grading our work. There's no teacher to set out a clearly defined syllabus of requirements. No deadlines. And definitely no "Student of the Month" award to earn.

For those seeking the approval of others through perfect performance, this lack of measurable success makes it hard to function. So we set *unreasonable* personal measures based on an ideal vision for ourselves. Only it's hard to know when we've met those expectations, if they're even possible to meet.

In school, we feared the disapproval of our teachers or our parents. But that was *somewhat* easy to manage when we knew the rules. Now we fear the disapproval of everyone, which drives us to make things perfect. This desire to make things perfect fuels our procrastination and we find ourselves following one of two patterns: either it's hard to start the work, or it's hard to finish.

You Can't Start

As I mentioned, I procrastinated on the writing of this book. It was amazing what other tasks I chose to do instead. They were all things I'd procrastinated on but apparently dreaded *less* than writing this book.

I scheduled a medical screening I'd put off for years, made a copy of a car key that required a special locksmith with a special machine, and decided to start exercising again.

But write? I was paralyzed by the thought of it. Seriously, why did I tackle a topic that only very intelligent people with lots of degrees and initials behind their name wrote on? I'm no expert! Who am I to write on a complicated subject like procrastination?

The more I researched the topic, the more I became so consumed over what to include in the book that I couldn't start. I didn't want to disappoint anyone. Visions of people thinking they'd wasted their money on this book just about made me sick.

Then it didn't help that I'm friends with someone who has had three books hit the *New York Times* bestseller list. Her last book was soaring to the top of the charts while I was trying to write mine. And although I know I shouldn't compare my success with hers, the impossibility of my writing a bestseller made me want to call my publisher to quit multiple times.

Finally, I had to admit I wasn't going to write a perfect book. And I'm not the perfect person to write on this subject. But I have been called by God to do it. So, since He is *much* smarter than me, I decided I'd better sit down at the computer, ask for His help, and start writing, trusting God to lead me.

This was not a one-and-done conversation I had with myself. Each chapter, I had to face that same high expectation and those same fears. What if I left out something important? What if I quoted a study that was debunked a year later only I didn't know it? What if a psychologist reads this and posts an angry comment on Amazon?

The perfectionist bully taunted me with dire consequences throughout the entire process of writing this book.

So how did I actually get it done? I chose to trust God. I know that sounds simple and maybe even cliché-ish. But it's really true.

As I mentioned earlier, years ago God challenged me to trust Him, not just say I trusted Him. What a difference it makes when I really trust God to direct and guide me!

Perfectionism directed my focus to the end result. But when I took my eyes off the results and put them on God, perfectionism lost its grip on me. No longer was the burden of the results squarely on my shoulders. I could include just what God wanted me to include.

Whew! What a relief it was—and is—to settle on this acceptance. So long as I depend on God for inspiration and direction, this book and any other I write will accomplish the purpose He set out. Just knowing God won't let me down gave me courage to start writing. And He'll do the same for you. His Word promises:

> Those who know your name trust in you,
>> for you, LORD, have never forsaken those who seek
>> you. (Ps. 9:10)

> Because of the LORD's great love we are not consumed,
>> for his compassions never fail.
> They are new every morning;
>> great is your faithfulness.
> I say to myself, "The LORD is my portion;
>> therefore I will wait for him." (Lam. 3:22–24)

> I will lead the blind by ways they have not known,
>> along unfamiliar paths I will guide them;
> I will turn the darkness into light before them
>> and make the rough places smooth.
> These are the things I will do;
>> I will not forsake them. (Isa. 42:16)

When we are faced with a challenging assignment, one where we doubt our ability to do it perfectly, we can choose to trust that

God will not fail us. That verse in Isaiah reminds me God will lead me in the unfamiliar path. The passage from Lamentations tells me God's help is fresh and available every day, even when I feel like I've really blown it the day before.

As you start to trust God and look for His direction, don't be surprised if you get confused over which "voice" in your heart is from God. My friend Kathi Lipp, coauthor of *The Cure for the "Perfect" Life*, suggests, "Ask whether you're being driven by fear or guided by God. The condemning voice in your head insisting, 'That's not good enough! Try harder!' is perfectionism. The still, small voice of loving conviction speaking to your heart is God."[2]

Assured of God's faithfulness and His love, we can proceed with confidence, giving the work our best efforts.

You Can't Finish

When my daughter Ruth was in third grade, she struggled to turn in her homework. Every time she sat down to work on it, she couldn't finish. She'd write and erase her answers so many times the paper would wear and rip in spots.

Her coloring pages suffered a similar fate. She'd sit at the kitchen table surrounded by little crumpled piles. Her pattern was always the same: she'd start with one color, change her mind, wad up the paper, and try again.

After much supervision on my part, I'd send her to school thinking her homework was done. Only then she'd second-guess herself and not turn it in. I imagine she pulled it out of her backpack and started erasing again.

Finally her teacher came to me with her concerns. "Ruth is a perfectionist and nothing is good enough to turn in," she said. "It's causing her a lot of anxiety."

The teacher's insight helped me understand my daughter better. Until then, I'd just been frustrated with what seemed like her lack of care for her work. That wasn't the problem at all. In fact, Ruth cared too much.

Once my eyes were opened, I could easily see the source of my daughter's desire to be perfect. Ruth has a desperate need to be accepted, and being "perfect" was her way to earn that acceptance.

Perhaps if Ruth had experienced acceptance at an early age, she wouldn't have felt this angst to work so hard for acceptance. But sadly, she didn't have that kind of unconditional love for the first eight years of her life.

My daughter didn't join our family through biology but rather through adoption. Ruth was born in the middle of a civil war in the African country of Liberia. She and her sister Cathrine experienced deprivation of every kind: no education, no electricity, no running water, and not enough food. They joined our family in 2005, when Ruth was eight and Cathrine ten.

The deprivation they experienced went beyond the physical. It was also cognitive and emotional. We'd seen this early on and had already been working with professional counselors to try to heal their deep wounds.

But those kinds of emotional wounds are hard to heal. And we're still working through them as a family.

Ruth doesn't have trouble starting but she has a deep aversion to finishing. She starts with optimism, psyches herself up, begins with gusto—then faces a challenge. Rather than finding a way to solve the problem, or a creative way around it, she slams to a stop. She's frustrated that her skills aren't perfect. She sees others accomplishing things and wants to be like them. But when her performance doesn't match her idea of perfection, she quits. To the best of our ability, we are helping our daughter see that to move forward she has to accept her particular set of circumstances as her starting point. She didn't choose them, and it isn't "fair." But it is reality.

I can relate to Ruth's resistance to finish, because that's hard for me too. But when the problem is perfectionism, what helps me press through and finish is to acknowledge that my best is always conditioned on my unique set of circumstances. In other words, I've got to play with the hand dealt me. Not with the hand I wish I had.

My "best" won't ever look like my neighbor's, my sister's, my friend's, or my coworker's best. I don't have their particular combination of natural and learned abilities. I'm not their age, I don't have their physique, nor do I have their personality. I'm wired and motivated differently. It helps to remind myself of these differences when discouragement makes me want to quit.

And it also helps me to realize that no matter my age or stage in life, there's still something I need to learn. Yes, God did equip me with a certain package deal of natural talent, but it all came in seed formation, needing to be nurtured and developed to reach the potential God intends for me.

When I embrace this idea of growth, perfectionism is left pouting on the sidewalk because I won't play its dangerous game.

Have a Growth Mindset versus a Fixed Mindset

Having a growth mindset allows us to accept our imperfections and see them as opportunities for improvement. Most perfectionists have a fixed mindset, however, which sees imperfections as failure. Stanford professor Carol Dwerk addresses these two mindsets in her book *Mindset*.

> Believing that your qualities are carved in stone—the fixed mindset—creates an urgency to prove yourself over and over. If you

have only a certain amount of intelligence, a certain personality, and a certain moral character—well, then you'd better prove that you have a healthy dose of them.[3]

In contrast, a growth mindset allows for mistakes and doesn't see them as a stamp of failure. Rather than trying to prove yourself, if you have a growth mindset you can say, "Why waste time proving over and over how great you are, when you could be getting better? Why hide deficiencies instead of overcoming them? . . . Why seek out the tried and true, instead of experiences that will stretch you?"[4]

A growth mindset is risky for a perfectionist. It means admitting we aren't perfect. Of course, everyone else already knew this! But now we can walk in that freedom.

And what a relief it is for me to admit my humanity. When I accept that I'm imperfect but able to learn and grow, I'm not threatened by a mistake. It's just a speed bump on my journey of improving, not a dead end. I don't need to detour around a challenge either; rather, I can welcome it as an opportunity to learn.

With this mindset, all those projects I've put off because I can't do them perfectly become less threatening. Will HGTV offer me a show of my own? Probably not, but I can enjoy the creativity of decorating without feeling like a failure.

A growth mindset allows me to embrace flexibility in all areas of my life, not rigid rules and results. Which not only helps me overcome perfectionism and procrastination but also helps me in being obedient to God's commands.

Embrace Flexibility

Blessed are the flexible, for they shall bend and not be broken.

I'm not sure who should get credit for that quote, but it's one to live by. And it's one the disciples of Jesus had to embrace, or they wouldn't have lasted long following a Savior who wasn't what they expected.

I imagine the disciples chose to follow Jesus with presupposed expectations of what He would be like. After all, like all good Jewish men, they'd grown up around rabbis. So not only did they expect Him to act like a rabbi but when He claimed to be God's Son they added expectations for Him as the Savior they'd been anticipating.

Had the disciples held tightly to those expectations, rejecting Jesus for who He was, they would have missed out on the wildness and beauty of God's grace, mercy, and forgiveness. When they abandoned their presuppositions, Jesus took the disciples on an adventure of faith they never anticipated. They experienced love and acceptance. They saw God's power. They were empowered themselves by the Holy Spirit. And they got a new definition of "perfect" when they met Jesus, who was perfect.

Yes, Jesus redefined "perfect." It was no longer something harsh and unforgiving. It was gracious and accepting. It welcomed outcasts and sinners and it rejected the prideful and legalistic. It was patient and kind and allowed itself to be interrupted by those in need.

When we hold ourselves to a standard of perfection we were never meant to meet, we too miss out on God's adventure of faith for us. And while God doesn't expect us to be perfect, we are called to be like Jesus in character. Which means being a lot more forgiving of ourselves and others.

Accept Yourself for Who You Are

I can't be perfect, but I can be perfectly me. And the more I'm me, with all my goofy, mixed-up parts, the better I am at it.

Rather than having perfection as our goal, could we make authenticity our goal? Could we strive to accept ourselves with the diverse set of strengths and weaknesses that make us uniquely us?

Walking in the freedom of being me, with my potential for growth and improvement intact, brings me peace and confidence. And these are not based on the perfection of my achievements but rather on God's perfect acceptance of me.

And the good news is this freedom is available for you too.

● PRACTICAL APPLICATION

Now that we've got an understanding of perfectionism's sneaky tactics, do you see it in your life? Are there things you have trouble starting or finishing because you fear your best isn't good enough? Would embracing a growth mindset rather than a fixed mindset help?

Consider the two areas you are working on. What do you need to learn in order to better manage this task and goal? Do you need to grow in your skills, experience, or character? Be specific and list what would help you excel.

My regular task:

My personal goal:

10

Replacing Bad Habits
with Good

My first instinct was to leave the clean, folded clothes on *top* of the dresser.

There was a logical reason. My arms were filled with other freshly laundered items, so it would have been difficult to open the drawer while balancing the stack. My plan was to come back a few minutes later when my arms were empty.

This impulse to stop short of finishing happens every day. In the morning. In the afternoon. In the evening. Especially when my days feel jam-packed and I want to move on to the next thing on my list as quickly as possible.

Which is why I want to leave clean clothes crumpled in a basket rather than folding them while they are still warm from the dryer. It's why I'd rather place dirty dishes on the counter than open the dishwasher and place them inside. And why I set the television remote on the end table rather than returning it to the decorative box I purchased so we'd never lose the remote again!

One day, when I draped my robe over the bathtub rim for the thousandth time, the irony of my choice hit me full force. Why would I not take three more steps to the closet and hang up my robe? Three steps! In just two seconds my robe would be in its place, hung on its hook on the back of the closet door.

In fact, why did I not just fold my pajamas and put them in the drawer? And put my curling iron under the sink? And make my bed? We're talking five minutes, max, and my bedroom would be picked up. Instead, my careless choices led to a very cluttered room.

I had developed a habit of not finishing what I started, and unfinished tasks surrounded me. And it wasn't all simple things like putting away clothes. My history of not finishing tasks included some major ones like leaving a wall half-painted. Recently my husband and I were looking at old photos and realized we had lived for years with a huge hole in the wall due to some rambunctious play on a recliner. We had the money to fix it; we just didn't. Quickly we became oblivious to it.

I had big goals for organizing my home and keeping it clean, but my daily habits were undermining my progress. I knew I had to change my habits, and I needed to start small. Obviously, all my big talk about getting organized wasn't making an impact on my behavior.

So I started hanging up my bathrobe every day. That was simple enough that I could do it. My bed was still unmade and the clothes were still on the dresser, but my robe was in its place.

Every time I wanted to toss that bathrobe on a horizontal surface, I said to myself, *Finish what you start!* Just that little cue made a difference. And enjoying a refreshingly cleaner room motivated me to keep up that habit, and eventually add others. Now it would drive me nuts to see my robe on the bathtub. But it took months of making a small, right choice to replace my bad habit.

Good habits are powerful tools for a procrastinator. When we get in the habit of doing something, we can't imagine not doing it.

Perhaps you have some routines that are second nature. I drink a cup of General Foods French vanilla coffee every day, and have for over twenty years. It's the first thing I do in the morning.

We really are creatures of habit. And over time, small repeated habits have a cumulative effect.

Addressing small bad habits can make a significant difference for those of us who struggle with procrastination. The thought of making huge, sweeping changes in my lifestyle intimidates me and I come to a screeching halt before I ever get started. But starting small? That seems manageable.

Not only do small beginnings motivate me to keep going, but they develop into good habits. And no matter how insignificant of an impact these seem to have on my big goals, they actually change the way my brain processes.

This is called neuroplasticity, and it's the brain's ability to change based on new experiences.

Laying Down Productive Mental Tracks

Neuroscientists are making fascinating discoveries about how the brain works, especially how it changes over time. We used to believe the brain stopped changing in adulthood. But researchers are discovering the brain has the power to change throughout our entire lives.

Our brains are constantly making neural pathways based on our behaviors. The more we persist in certain habits, the stronger those pathways become, which is why we say things like "practice makes perfect." What that really means is practice makes stronger neural pathways.

The best visual of neural pathways I can think of is of sledding down a snow-covered hill. The first time you head down the hill you have multiple options. But the more you go down the same path, the deeper that track will be.

When people feel locked in a bad habit, they might say they are "stuck in a rut." And that's literally what's happening in their brains. Burka and Yuen put it this way: "The brain is always changing. The good news is that it can generate new, flexible behavior. The bad news is that it can also strengthen old, rigid behaviors."[1]

It's not just behaviors that become habits, it's also our thinking—where procrastination starts for all of us. *I'll start tomorrow. I'll feel more like facing this task next week. I'm sure I'll have enough time to finish over the weekend.*

Each time we allow our thoughts to follow the pattern of procrastination, we reaffirm those wrong thoughts and deepen the neural pathway. Can't you just see how our procrastination is a habit that gets strengthened each time we do it?

Fortunately, the opposite is also true. We have the ability to bravely face our procrastination and make lasting changes.

How Habits Develop

Our understanding of habits is relatively new. It wasn't until the early 1990s that scientists realized the brain's ability to remember a habit is a unique function, one independent of memory.

Habit routines are stored in the center of the brain, where our automatic behaviors such as breathing, swallowing, and fear response are controlled. Specifically, this area is called the basal ganglia.[2]

In one study, scientists put tiny probes in rats' brains to monitor cognitive activity while the rats ran through a maze that ended with a treat. The first time through the maze the rats' brains were exploding with activity, especially in the basal ganglia. But each time the rats ran the maze successfully, their brain activity diminished until there was very little response at all. The rats were running on autopilot.

The sequence of the rats' actions turned into a routine, which became a habit. The same thing happens to us. This switch from high activity to low allows our brains to reserve energy and function efficiently. As researchers continued to study this pattern, they identified a three-step process for all habits.

First there is the cue, which tells the brain to switch to the learned habit. Second is the routine, which can be a behavior, thought, or emotion. Third is the reward. Also added to the habit loop is a craving that develops for the reward, which is why bad habits are so hard to break.

But the good news is we can change our habits. It will take conscious effort, but it is possible. According to Charles Duhigg, author of *The Power of Habit*:

> To change a habit, you must keep the old cue, and deliver the old reward, but insert a new routine. That's the rule: If you used the same cue, and provide the same reward, you can shift the routine and change the habit. Almost any behavior can be transformed if the cue and reward stay the same.[3]

Creating New Tracks of Behavior

Let's take a look at how this applies to overcoming our bad procrastination habits. The reward for a procrastinator is the relief from not having to deal with the unpleasant task. Obviously that's not a healthy reward, but it is a reward.

The challenge is to rewrite the routine so we feel the same relief—only we experience it because we've accomplished the task.

The cues for a procrastinator might be physical, but my guess is yours, like mine, are mental. My cue that a procrastination choice is about to happen is the thought, *I'll do that later.* My routine is a redirection of my thoughts toward a different task. And my craving is for the reward of relief.

This is what happened with my bathrobe habit. The cue was my thought to hang it up later, my new routine was to actually hang it up, and I replaced the relief of not doing the task with the relief that it was done.

I've successfully addressed other bad habits, one at a time, using this practice. There are still more to go, but success builds upon success. And I have confidence in my ability to change my habits. Not all at once, but one at a time.

Creating New Mental Tracks of Truth

Our mental tracks of discouragement are perhaps even more difficult to overcome than our behavior patterns. Words spoken over us, or words we've spoken to ourselves, have the power to lock us in patterns of defeat and shame that keep us chained to the procrastination cycle.

In order to break these mental habits, we must catch our devaluing mental scripts the moment they start and replace them with the truth. This is why Scripture memorization is so powerful.

The Bible says we "have been born again, not of perishable seed, but of imperishable, through the living and enduring word of God" (1 Pet. 1:23), and "the word of God is living and active, sharper than any two-edged sword, piercing to the division of soul and of spirit, of joints and of marrow, and discerning the thoughts and intentions of the heart" (Heb. 4:12 ESV).

When an old thought pattern tempts us, we must immediately have a verse of truth to replace it.

My friend Renee Swope, author of *A Confident Heart*, knows how to defeat the lies of the enemy with God's Word. In one chapter of her book, she offers Bible verses to memorize when self-defeating thoughts arise.[4] Here are some that will help defeat procrastination:

When I Say	God Says	Powerful Promises
I can't figure things out.	I will direct your steps.	"Trust in the LORD with all your heart and lean not on your own understanding; in all your ways submit to him, and he will make your paths straight." (Prov. 3:5–6)
This situation is impossible.	All things are possible with My help.	"What is impossible with man is possible with God." (Luke 18:27)
I can't do it.	Rely on My strength and you can do all that I've called you to do.	"I have strength for all things in Christ Who empowers me." (Phil. 4:13 AMPC)
I feel over-whelmed.	I will give you peace.	"I have told you these things, so that in Me you may have [perfect] peace and confidence." (John 16:33 AMPC)
I don't have enough confidence.	I will be your confidence.	"For the LORD will be your con-fidence and will keep your foot from being caught." (Prov. 3:26 NASB)
I'm not strong enough.	I am your strength.	"God is the strength of my heart and my portion forever." (Ps. 73:26)
I'll never change.	I am transforming you.	"And we all, who with unveiled faces contemplate the Lord's glory, are being transformed into his image with ever-increasing glory, which comes from the Lord, who is the Spirit." (2 Cor. 3:18)

Let this be just the start of your truth toolbox. Every time a negative thought arises, use it as a cue to research the truth about what God says about you. If you aren't familiar with how to research Scripture, you can go to Biblegateway.com or Cross walk.com and do a keyword search. Or you might try one of my favorite websites, OpenBible.info, and use their topical Bible.

Strengthening Our Starting Muscles

My daughter Cathrine is built to run. Her legs are strong and fast. She excels at soccer and a few years ago decided to try track.

She faithfully went to practice and walked off the track each day having given it her all. But in spite of her speed, she never finished well. Finally I spoke to the coach because I couldn't understand how she could be so fast yet not perform as well as everyone expected.

He said, "Cathrine will do well when she learns to get off the starting block well."

I understood. It was awkward for her to bend over with feet at an angle and planted in the pedals. She was used to pushing off the ground, not a metal block. And as Cathrine learned to start more efficiently, her times indeed improved.

Starting a task or project can be a challenge for a procrastinator. But the only way we strengthen our starting muscles is to *start*. Then do it again and again.

If you have trouble starting, consider it a muscle you can strengthen. Imagine yourself getting stronger each time you start. Don't worry about how long you keep at the task. Celebrate the fact that you got started!

Our Model for Finishing Well

Finishing well requires discipline that doesn't come naturally. But it's key to living a life that's managable and reflects God's priorities. And while books on time management and productivity can help, our best role model for finishing well is Jesus.

Jesus is the picture of focus and discipline, especially in the midst of many people demanding His attention. In the book of John we read about a time when Jesus sat by a well while His disciples went for food. While He waited, a solitary woman came to draw water and Jesus engaged her in a life-changing conversation. Jesus's words not only transformed this woman's life, but she went and told her whole village about the man she had met.

On this day, Jesus could have pleaded exhaustion or frustration. He'd been traveling, it was warm, and He was hungry. Not only that, but this was a Samaritan woman, a race of people the Jews despised. And this particular woman was an outcast from even her own people.

Just one of those reasons would have been enough for me to pretend my attention was on something else. I would not have been in the mood to strike up a conversation in the middle of a day like that.

But not Jesus. In spite of all the reasons why He might have ignored her, Jesus narrowed His focus and turned His full attention to this woman.

He finished the assignment God gave Him.

When He reunited with His disciples, they tried to get Him to eat.

> But he said to them, "I have food to eat that you know nothing about."
>
> Then his disciples said to each other, "Could someone have brought him food?"
>
> "My food," said Jesus, "is to do the will of him who sent me and to finish his work. Don't you have a saying, 'It's still four months until harvest'? I tell you, open your eyes and look at the fields! They are ripe for harvest." (John 4:32–35)

Jesus knew what His Father had asked Him to do and He was committed to "finish" His work. Jesus saw the reward of the harvest and persevered through personal discomfort.

And I'm eternally glad Jesus didn't give up on finishing His work. Because of His sacrifice, we have the gift of eternal life.

Changing lifelong habits will take time. But it is possible. Just take them one at a time. With God's truth to guide us and His strength to empower us, we can replace bad habits with good.

PRACTICAL APPLICATION

Did you identify any of your bad habits when I shared some of mine? It's so easy to get into the habit of putting off things that would take just a few minutes to complete. By themselves, small undone tasks aren't harmful. But bad habits tend to multiply and have a cumulative effect.

What good habits would make a difference as you tackle your regular task and personal goal? Identify one good habit you can begin today.

My regular task:

My personal goal:

11

Strengthening Willpower

Have you ever had the best of intentions to eat a salad for dinner? Maybe you've shopped for the tomatoes and cucumber, even splurged on some croutons. You fully intend to eat healthy that evening.

Then your day turned stressful with problems at work. The school called because your daughter forgot her lunch. Plus, the dog got out and the neighbors left an angry message telling you to keep your pet under control. Really? You can barely keep yourself under control!

As a day like that comes to a close, what is the very last thing you want to eat for dinner? Salad! Right?

Just give me something with lots of melted cheese! And sausage and mushrooms. On a thick crust with chunky marinara sauce. After solving problems, readjusting my schedule, and overcoming frustration, I want something comforting. Something that brings me joy and happiness to eat. I have no willpower left to eat a salad.

Willpower, our ability to resist self-gratification for a greater goal, is a prized resource. If we only had more willpower, we are certain we could change the troublesome areas of our lives.

Ask anyone who has ever tried to diet about the importance of willpower. As soon as you boldly declare you are going to diet, and you really mean it this time, willpower packs up and leaves.

But it's not just dieting. Willpower is needed for any positive change we want to make in our lives. Studies show that we all want more willpower in our lives. The American Psychological Association's annual "Stress in America" survey asks participants about their ability to make healthy changes in their lives. Not surprisingly, lack of willpower is regularly listed as the number one reason for not following through with positive changes.[1]

Willpower helps us keep working on a boring but important task when we'd rather check Facebook. It makes our fingers press the off button on the TV remote and grab a dust rag. And it motivates us to start work on pursuing our dreams when it's easier to accept the status quo.

The ability to control our thoughts, words, and actions is a powerful indicator of success in all areas of life. We need it to reject false thoughts and keep them from taking root, to refrain from saying unkind things, to speak the truth, and to have the power to do the right thing at the right time. When we give in to self-defeating behaviors, we sabotage ourselves.

Procrastinators understand this self-sabotage better than most. We miss out on opportunities, live with chaos of our own making, and carry the guilt of it all. We know we should take positive steps toward completing tasks but we feel powerless to do so. We live with the sadness of intentionally delaying that which is in our best interest to do now.

For a procrastinator, willpower is elusive, showing up at unexpected times and being MIA when we need it most.

Are some people born with more willpower?

Researchers believe that some people *are* born with a stronger sense of willpower than others. In the famous "Marshmallow Test" conducted by Walter Mischel and Ebbe B. Ebbesen at Stanford University in 1970, researchers studied how children responded when offered a treat. The children were set in a room with a treat of some kind, often a marshmallow, and told if they waited to eat it, they could have a second treat. Out of the over six hundred children who took the test, one-third delayed gratification long enough to get a second treat.[2] The promise of a second marshmallow wasn't enough to deter the other two-thirds from immediately enjoying the single treat.

Researchers then followed up with these children through the years, and the results were consistent. The children with higher willpower in the first test continued to show greater self-control through the years, resulting in higher educational achievements and better overall health.

One of these follow-up studies involved tracking down fifty-nine subjects of the marshmallow test.[3] As part of the research, they performed MRIs on these individuals and discovered that the prefrontal cortex (the center of our executive processing) was more active in those with greater willpower. Conversely, the MRI showed more activity in the ventral striatum (a region thought to process desires and rewards) in those with lower self-control.

Science can't tell why there's such a difference in our brains, but those of us who believe in an intentional Creator know this isn't an accident. However, God certainly didn't intend for some to be better able to withstand temptation than others. That would mean He shrugged His shoulders and left the rest of the world on its own.

I believe God strengthens our brains differently for different purposes. We are all strong in some areas and weak in others. We may not know all the reasons for God's choices, but we can trust He has our good in mind.

Although many procrastinators find it harder to employ will-power, and give in quicker to marshmallows or whatever the temptation might be, we all can learn techniques to increase our willpower.

Two Steps of Willpower

Willpower seems to have two steps. The first is to resist temptation and the second is to press toward a goal. We need willpower to do both.

If we only resist temptation but don't move forward, we are standing still. If we try to move forward without turning from temptation, we will stumble back. For example, if I'm determined to eat healthier foods, I have to stop eating junk food first. If I want to keep paper clutter off my counters, I have to stop stacking up mail.

Whenever we want to make a positive change in our lives, there is always a two-step process of stopping the old habit and starting the new one. Sometimes those two things happen quickly and seamlessly, but other times we must address them individually.

Step One: Say No to Temptation

Most of us have trouble doing the right thing in some areas of our lives. We may be superstars in keeping clutter at bay but let dirty laundry pile up. We may keep our offices spotless but our homes are a disaster. Sometimes we just don't have the energy to do what we know we should do, and we give in to something easier or more pleasant.

This doesn't mean we're heathen; it means we're human. The Bible calls this giving in to temptation, and we all face it. First Corinthians 10:13 says, "No temptation has overtaken you except what is common to mankind." We all are tempted to give in to the same self-gratifying choices. Paul, the author of 1 Corinthians, used the Israelites as examples of those who gave in to idolatry, sexual immorality, testing Christ, and grumbling, with devastating consequences.

Satan even tried to get Jesus to give in by tempting Him with food, testing God, and power. Even though Jesus didn't give in to Satan's taunts, the Bible says He was tempted: "Because he himself suffered when he was tempted, he is able to help those who are being tempted" (Heb. 2:18).

Even those closest to Jesus gave in to temptation. Before Jesus was betrayed, He asked His disciples to stand watch while He prayed. After praying He returned to find His disciples asleep, and admonished Peter by saying, "Watch and pray so that you will not fall into temptation. The spirit is willing, but the flesh is weak" (Matt. 26:41).

Temptations come in many forms for a procrastinator. In fact, there's not much that won't tempt us from doing what we know we should do and have the power to do. The problem with temptation, for a procrastinator, is the object of our desire isn't always an obvious sin. If it were, it would be so much easier to address.

If I put off cleaning my kitchen to rob a bank, the temptation is pretty obvious. But if I really need to clean my kitchen and instead I decide to go shopping, well, that's not such an obvious problem. I might even be able to justify that shopping was needed.

When I don't want to do something, everything else looks tempting. But whether or not I'm tempted to sin or to distraction, God understands. He knows our human natures are frail and we will be led astray by our weaknesses. The second part of 1 Corinthians 10:13 provides the hope we need to avoid temptation: "And God is faithful; he will not let you be tempted beyond what you can bear. But when you are tempted, he will also provide a way out so that you can endure it."

What does this "way out" look like? It's different for every situation. But God will provide it if we look for it. The important thing for us is to be aware that we are being tempted.

The next time you feel resistance to complete a task, press the pause button. Is there something that's tempting you away from it? There might not be; sometimes we just don't want to do something. But if you are faced with two options and one tempts you away from the other, ask God for that escape route.

You might find a Scripture verse pops into your head, or hear His voice speaking encouragement to your heart. Or it might be something like a well-timed text or phone call. Trust that God will help you say no to temptation.

The other tool God has given us to face temptation is His Word. When Satan tempted Jesus, Jesus quoted Scripture. The truth of God's Word nullifies the lie wrapped in the temptation. Jesus Himself said, "If you hold to my teaching, you are really my disciples. Then you will know the truth, and the truth will set you free" (John 8:31–32).

The only truth that sets us free is the truth we know. Which is why we must arm ourselves with the Word of God as we face procrastination.

We can start with the Scripture verses Jesus used and build on that to create our own library of temptation-facing truth.

> "Man does not live on bread alone but on every word that comes from the mouth of the LORD." (Deut. 8:3)
>
> "Do not put the LORD your God to the test." (6:16)
>
> "Fear the LORD your God, serve him only." (6:13)

What's your temptation? Gossip? Idleness? Gluttony? Take some time to research verses on these topics, write them down, and memorize them. Then when temptation strikes, you'll be ready.

Creating a Mental Image

Another tool to strengthen your willpower is to create an unpleasant association with what you want to avoid. Walter Mischel, the founder of the original marshmallow test, continued to study the idea of willpower and those who seemed to have more of it. As Mischel interviewed the test's children throughout the years, he learned that a consistent and crucial factor in delaying gratification involves changing your perception of the object you want to resist.

By creating a mental image that distances us from what we want, we are learning to mentally "cool" what Mischel calls the "hot" aspects of our environment, or those things that pull us away from our goals. Mischel himself struggled with smoking and tried for years to stop. It wasn't until he saw a very ill lung cancer patient in the hospital that he was able to stop. From that moment on, whenever he wanted a cigarette he created a picture in his mind of this patient. He was able to stop smoking immediately.[4]

Could we apply this mental technique to our procrastination? To do so, we need to identify the choices we make that keep us from completing our tasks or reaching our goals. This technique won't apply to everything we procrastinate on, but when there's an obvious source of temptation, try assigning a mental image to it.

Do you tend to pick up fast food rather than prepare a healthy meal? Imagine the golden arches are actually clogged arteries. Do you find the couch more appealing than a walk? Imagine your rear end becoming as big as the cushion. Do you put off spending time resting and reenergizing? Imagine yourself as a stressed-out, impatient woman no one wants to be around.

Reducing Decision Making and Increasing Mental Energy

Have you ever been mentally exhausted after shopping? It's not the physical effort of walking the mall that's tough. It's all those choices. Researchers are discovering that making decisions saps your mental energy and can weaken your willpower. (Which could explain why some people overspend.)

Maybe you've experienced this if you've spent time with a six-year-old lately. They have an endless supply of questions. Can we go to McDonald's? Can I wear my bathing suit to church? Can we get a puppy? Can I have a cookie?

In a very short time, Mom is exhausted and either says no or yes to everything. We've all been there and just given in. Which is why it can make complete sense to have Pop-Tarts for dinner or allow a child to wear a Superman cape to school.

The more decisions we have to make, the less stamina we have to make the best one for us at that moment. Which is why at the end of a stressful day, I could eat half a pizza. Or even a whole one on a really bad day.

Please tell me I'm not the only one who has zoned out in a store. I once left Hobby Lobby in tears because I could not pick the right tie-dye kit for my daughter. I already felt inadequate as a crafter, and the number of options just did me in.

We have more freedom with our money and time than generations before us, and yet that very freedom limits us. Choices, although a blessing, can be a burden to our overtaxed minds. And the numerous alternatives that should empower us actually hinder us from getting things done.

Researchers are discovering that making too many decisions impairs our self-control, which is a much-needed resource for a procrastinator.[5] In a 2008 study led by Kathleen Vohs from the University of Michigan, researchers hypothesized that decision making depletes the same resource used for self-control and active responding. In four different experiments, participants were assigned to groups that either made choices or didn't. The choices were simple, such as choosing between two different shirts, scented candles, or shampoo brands. Each group had an assignment but only one group had to make decisions.

Then each group was given a different assignment that rated their ability to sustain an unpleasant task completely unrelated to the first test. For example, in one experiment the participants had to drink an unpleasant-tasting beverage after their task. The group whose first task did not involve making decisions drank significantly more of the distasteful beverage than their decision-making counterparts.

The findings were consistent in all four experiments: making decisions reduced subsequent self-control. The authors of the study wrote this summary:

> The present findings suggest that self-regulation, active initiative, and effortful choosing draw on the same psychological resource. Making decisions depletes that resource, thereby weakening the subsequent capacity for self-control and active initiative.[6]

This research explains so much. I'm sure we've all experienced this phenomenon but haven't known why. So now that we know even decision making unrelated to our procrastination can affect willpower, what are we going to do about it?

Transposing Easy and Hard Work

If decision making taxes our self-regulation, then an easy response is to minimize decisions before tackling something we've been procrastinating.

This requires a paradigm shift in our approach to work. It's common for me to put off hard projects until later in the day. My philosophy has been to get smaller tasks out of the way so my plate is empty. I reason that I'll have a fresh mind when I turn to that "big" project I've been avoiding.

Plus, I like checking things off my to-do list. It gives me a sense of accomplishment.

However, by the time I've worked through emails or whatever "small" tasks I face first, I've no energy or willpower left to work on the hard stuff. So I put it off until tomorrow, determined to work on it then.

You can imagine what "tomorrow" looks like when I follow the same pattern of doing small tasks first.

Brian Tracy, author of *Eat That Frog!*, understands the importance of addressing the hard work first. He says, "The key to reaching high levels of performance and productivity is to develop the lifelong habit of tackling your major task first thing in the morning."[7]

You may not be able to finish your most important task in one morning, but the habit of starting on it first thing will make a huge impact on how you feel about yourself. Plus, if your other work isn't as difficult, you won't need to use your freshest reservoir of willpower to accomplish it.

Planning in Advance

Another way to maximize willpower is to minimize the little decisions we make throughout the week by planning in advance. What area of your life would benefit from a bit of preplanning? Could you preplan your breakfasts, what you wear, what your kids will have for lunch, and what days you will go to the gym? By taking some time each weekend to write out a simple plan for the upcoming week, you could avoid some decisions and eliminate stress in the process.

Establishing routines will help reduce decision making as well. A morning routine is especially powerful in starting the day right. When my children were younger, our mornings were chaotic. After lots of trial and error trying to find the right combination of rules,

I decided to put everyone on a timed schedule—including myself. This included wake-up time, what time everyone needed to be in the kitchen for breakfast, what time we needed to be dressed, and what time we would leave the house. And the order simplified everything.

As you think about preplanning and setting routines, don't forget to take care of yourself. Too many women neglect themselves as they serve their families and others. Make sure you predecide how to care for you! This might mean scheduling a walk with a friend, a trip to the salon, or a bubble bath.

Step Two: Motivation to Press On

Sometimes we can effectively deal with those things that deplete our willpower, like decision making, and still not have what it takes to move forward. When that happens, it's helpful to understand our own motivations and use them to our advantage.

I came to a deeper understanding of my personal motivations when I learned of the Motivational DNA Test created by Tamara Lowe, the cofounder of Get Motivated Seminars, Inc. and author of *Get Motivated!* I took the free online test, not expecting to learn anything new about myself as I'm pretty predictable when it comes to personality tests. But this test was unlike any I'd taken before, and my results were surprising. Not so much in how I was motivated, but in what doesn't motivate me (to take this test yourself, go to http://www.motivatedbythebook.com/Test.aspx).

Lowe has discovered we are motivated in three main ways:

Drives: The internal forces that move us to action

Needs: What we need to feel fulfilled

Awards: What we desire for our achievement

Within each of these three areas, there are two distinct motivators:

Drives: Connection and Production

Needs: Stability and Variety

Awards: Internal and External

To some extent, we can be motivated by all six of these factors. But Lowe proposes that each of us has a preference. And when we understand our preferences, we can use them wisely.

> As you begin to consciously motivate yourself in the way that you were designed to be motivated, you will experience remarkable advancements in your career and personal life. Goals that eluded you in the past will be accomplished with ease.[8]

After taking the test, I learned my "Motivational DNA" consists of production, stability, and internal. As I mentioned, these weren't surprising. I know I'm project oriented and don't need many pats on the back. But what did surprise me was the comparison of production to connection. I'd never seen those two motivations as opposites.

As I considered this test and how it related to procrastination, I realized I procrastinate on projects that are relational in nature. It's not that I don't care, but these projects don't have immediate rewards such as checking something off a to-do list. This explained to me why I resist participating in any kind of social media. I can't wrap it up in a project and produce some kind of product.

I've had to look for ways to build motivation into my work to avoid procrastinating on those things that don't naturally motivate me.

How might you use information like this? If you are motivated by connection and external awards, perhaps you could reward yourself with time with a friend upon completion of an unpleasant task.

Or if you're like me and resist projects where you can't see results, can you create some definition—like time—and see that as a product? For example, you might set a goal of thirty minutes of work and see if that motivates you. Understanding our unique makeup is always enjoyable, and when we can use it to overcome weak areas in our lives, like procrastination, it's a double blessing.

Willpower or His Power?

With all the practical tools we have to increase our willpower, they pale in comparison to the gift of strength God offers us in Christ.

The apostle Paul experienced this strength and wrote to the church in Corinth about it. Paul was a man proud of his background, and before meeting Jesus he would have boasted of his own power. And yet after meeting Jesus Christ and choosing to follow Him, Paul realized his own strength was puny in comparison to Christ's.

As much as I want to appear strong in my own strength, I'm desperately aware of my weakness. And like Paul, I'm learning to accept that I'm nothing without Christ. It's then, when I admit I'm bankrupt, that Christ's power is revealed. I may be able to accomplish some things on my own, but that which is highest and best requires a strength I can't manifest within myself. No amount of willpower can compare to God's power.

Here's how the apostle Paul puts it, speaking of Jesus:

> But he said to me, "My grace is sufficient for you, for my power is made perfect in weakness." Therefore I will boast all the more gladly about my weaknesses, so that Christ's power may rest on me. That is why, for Christ's sake, I delight in weaknesses, in

insults, in hardships, in persecutions, in difficulties. For when I am weak, then I am strong. (2 Cor. 12.9 10)

As we face our own procrastination, we would be foolish to try to conquer it in our own strength. May we accept our weaknesses and even delight in them, inviting Christ to be our strength. There's nothing else that even comes close.

● PRACTICAL APPLICATION

In this chapter we discussed the idea of willpower. We need will-power to avoid temptation and to motivate us to do the right thing. Consider the two areas you are working on. Do you find yourself tempted to do something else when you think about starting your work? Is there a way you can increase your motivation by incorporating your unique design? How can you make positive strides in this area?

My regular task:

My personal goal:

12

Becoming a
Wise Time Manager

Managing time seems to be at the heart of procrastination. We all want to know how to stretch time or make it speed up. Personally, I'd like to add a few hours to my day.

Interestingly, we each have a unique perception of time. And it changes throughout our lives. When we are children, time seems to drag. Christmas and birthdays take forever to arrive. Then our teen years and twenties go by in a flash. Small children take us back to the long days, but in hindsight they were too short. And late nights waiting for a teenager to come home make late nights with a crying baby seem like a cinch.

We either love the passing of time or we resent it. Some hate the wasting of it, and live with regrets of not making the most of it. And we all seem to wish we used it more wisely.

Here's the reality about how we use time: we will never drift into managing time well. We won't one day wake up to find ourselves using time wisely and efficiently. Most of us struggle to figure out *what* we are supposed to do with our time and *when* we are supposed to do it. And are looking for help wherever we can get it.

I have met some people, usually the ones I admire most, who are acutely aware of the value of time. They know their priorities and make choices that reflect them. But this didn't happen automatically. It took commitment for them to change and to be realistic about their time.

A Procrastinator's Relationship with Time

Procrastinators have a creative relationship with time. That's a nice way of saying we have an *unrealistic* view of time. But of course, you already know that.

Actually, we all have our own experience with time. This is called "subjective time." As we all know, sometimes time flies, especially when we are having fun. And other times it feels like the old adage, "A watched pot never boils."

Cultural differences also affect subjective time. A number of years ago I traveled to Ecuador with Compassion International. We toured the Compassion project and family homes with both an American guide and an Ecuadorian guide.

At one point we split into two groups with the plan to meet back at the bus at 1:00 p.m. Our in-country guide took half of us into the home of a family with sponsored children. We sat in their humble home as our Ecuadorian guide helped translate our conversation with the family. At 12:50, our American guide thanked the family for the visit and escorted the group outside. But the in-country guide stayed behind and kept talking.

Time was ticking, and our group realized we would be late getting to the bus. Checking and rechecking our watches only made us more anxious. Our American guide, who'd made this trip many times, seemed unruffled. He smiled and explained, "Ecuadorians run their day by relationships while Americans run their day by the clock."

This interpretation of time wasn't wrong. It worked for them. And it might even work for you at times. However, conflict arises because most of us live in a nation where businesses and schools and churches are run on objective time, which is also called "clock time."

The goal isn't to eliminate subjective time. We can't possibly do that. Nor would we want to make everyone slaves of the clock. Personally, I'm charmed by those who can prioritize relationships over projects.

The ideal approach is for us to respect clock time and integrate it gracefully into subjective time. This would enable us to accurately gauge how long it will take to accomplish a task, like run to the grocery store. We would know when to put down a book in order to leave to get to work on time. And when to start working on that project due in a month.

It sounds so simple. But just watching the clock isn't always a solution. Sometimes a procrastinator is so deeply rooted in subjective time they don't see their understanding of time as the problem. They falsely think there is always more time. Hence the last-minute dash to the finish line. And the missed deadlines and opportunities.

When a procrastinator stubbornly resists working within the reality of objective time, procrastination becomes a chronic problem, not just an annoyance. It causes conflict at home and at work and compounds stressful situations.

If this section is hitting close to home, perhaps it's time to confront your wishful thinking when it comes to time. We cannot outsmart time, only respect it and work within its constraints.

Procrastinators, as we have observed, prefer to remain in the vague realms of potential and possibility and do not like to be concrete, measured, or limited. When they are ultimately caught short of time, they are surprised, disappointed, and even offended.[1]

If we are to confront procrastination in our lives, we must be honest about our subjective view of time. Refusing to accept objective time creates an illusion of control. And what a dangerous illusion it is! Only God has control over time; we are but managers of the time He has given us.

And as managers, we should use time wisely. There are a few techniques I have found that have helped me become a better manager of my time, and hopefully some of these will help you as well.

Schedule Uninterrupted Time

Whether you're a mom caring for children or an executive managing a business—or both—uninterrupted time doesn't happen often. Someone always needs something.

And when we are working on something that requires focus and creativity, interruptions are difficult. They require us to stop, redirect our attention, respond, and then redirect our attention back to our original work. This uses time and mental energy. And for a procrastinator, interruptions can be an excuse to stop working.

What could your mind do without the threat of an email, text, or phone call? Want to find out?

The next time you have an important project due or a difficult task, try making an appointment with yourself, and put it on your calendar. Block out an hour and let others know you are booked and unavailable during that time. You don't have to explain or apologize. We're all used to people having appointments, and understand that a phone call or email will be returned later.

Do you worry that people will need to reach you? Consider Jeff Bezos, founder and CEO of Amazon. He knows the importance of unscheduled time and plans it into his week. In the early years of starting Amazon, Bezos tried to keep his schedule completely open on Mondays and Thursdays just to allow himself time to think or to explore an idea.

If the founder of the biggest online shopping mall in the world can keep two full days to himself, we can probably find a few hours. Plan for it, then turn off your phone, shut down your email, and remove anything else that will distract you from your purpose.

Beware the sneaky siren of catch-up work. When we have uninterrupted time, there is a tendency to use that time to catch up on something. My go-to catch-up job is responding to emails. Maybe catch-up work for you is laundry, phone calls, or errands. But don't start anything except your important task! If you say to yourself, *I'll just answer a few emails first,* you will get sucked into the black hole of email and you'll squander all of your precious time.

Since most of us are unused to uninterrupted time, it might be hard to focus at first. We are conditioned to hearing the ding of an incoming text and are on alert, waiting for it. Start with small blocks of time, even fifteen minutes, and work your way up from there. With practice, you will strengthen your ability to focus.

Identify Time Wasters

My friend Karen Ehman often has people ask her how she's able to do so much. She's highly productive and I'm amazed by her as well. Her answer to those who ask is always the same: "You don't see what I *don't* do."

Karen lives her priorities better than most other women I know. As important as what she chooses to do is what she says no to. Such as watching TV. Oh, she'll sit down with her husband and sons when a game is on, but that's more to spend time with them while doing something they love.

Karen doesn't work like a crazy woman either. She writes and speaks professionally and works part-time from home, but loving people is her priority and she makes choices with her time so that she's available.

We'd see these same types of hard choices being made if we were able to watch the most productive women in the world go about their days. We'd see them minimize distractions and time stealers in order to make time for what matters most.

Every choice of how to spend our time has an opportunity cost. "Opportunity cost" is a term used in economics to identify the benefit, profit, or value of what is given up to achieve or obtain something else. This cost is used when computing the cost-benefit analysis of a project.[2]

For example, the opportunity cost of going to college is the money we would have made had we gone right into a job. The opportunity cost of watching television all Saturday is the housework we might have done.

If we want to manage our time well, we need to count the opportunity cost when we engage in what could be a time waster. And today we have more potential time wasters than ever before. They are traps in our day, waiting to snare us and redirect our attention away from our priorities.

It's not that they are detrimental on their own. But they become problems when they keep us from achieving our goals.

Here's a personal example. I find that reading a magazine is a great way to get inspired. I love home decorating and cooking magazines. However, if I'm facing a deadline or my children have asked for help, it can become a time stealer. Unless I'm reading for research or I've scheduled a break, I should postpone my reading pleasure until an appropriate moment.

Be honest about what is stealing your time from your priorities. Some things will be obvious, others are harder to identify. It's a little like starting to budget your finances. Say you start the week with a hundred dollars, but by the end of the week you have no money and nothing to show for it. Where did all that money go? Time is just like that. If you have no idea where your time goes, keep a time journal for a week. Write down what you do all day, and after a week you'll see some patterns.

Here are a few common time wasters:

Obvious

- Television
- Social media
- Surfing the internet
- Phone calls
- Online games
- Interruptions
- Disorganized meetings

Not-So-Obvious

- Tasks you could have delegated
- Indecision
- Requests from others
- Unclear communication
- Unclear objectives and priorities
- Lack of planning
- Stress and fatigue
- Personal disorganization
- Crisis management
- Unhealthy friendships
- Worry

Once you've identified your personal time wasters, consider their opportunity cost. Then, next time you have a choice about what to do, you'll be equipped to choose more wisely.

The Importance of Time to Plan

Taking time to plan your day, or even your week, is one of the most undervalued uses of time. Every minute we spend planning saves as many as ten minutes in execution.[3] What an investment! Just ten minutes spent identifying our priorities for the day, picking which tasks to complete, and setting the order of those tasks could save us an hour and a half of wasted time.

Getting into the habit of planning helps me think and work proactively rather than reactively. Reactive work puts me at the mercy of the agendas and needs of others. Proactive work isn't selfish; rather, it makes us good stewards of the responsibilities God has assigned to us. First Corinthians 4:2 says, "Now it is required that those who have been given a trust must prove faithful." Planning helps us be trustworthy.

The Bible affirms the importance of planning, with verses such as, "Good planning and hard work lead to prosperity, but hasty shortcuts lead to poverty" (Prov. 21:5 NLT). But at the same time we are warned to make sure to submit our plans to the Lord: "Commit to the LORD whatever you do, and he will establish your plans" (Prov. 16:3).

Before I plan, I always start with reading my Bible. This sets my mind on the Lord's will and reminds me that He is sovereign over my life, my time, and my plans. I pray a simple prayer: *Lord, show me what You want me to do today.* Then I trust Him to show me.

I don't wait for a neon light to flash to show me God's will for my day. The Bible assures us God will give us direction one way or another. Proverbs 3:5–6 says:

> Trust in the LORD with all your heart
>   and lean not on your own understanding;
> in all your ways submit to him,
>   and he will make your paths straight.

Once my heart is right, I consider all the work on my project and task lists and the deadlines for each of them. Then I look at the week ahead and what commitments I already have. Finally, I assign certain tasks to certain days. This is very helpful when I've got a project with multiple steps. There's something so motivating about knowing I'm making progress, step by step.

On a daily basis, remember to put your most important tasks first on your agenda. This will make the most of your willpower, energy, and focus. Guard your morning time jealously and put off smaller, less mentally taxing work until later in the day.

The most practical and helpful thing I've realized is that I get significantly *less* done in a day than I wish. So I only set a goal of accomplishing two or three larger items a day. Then if the day goes smoothly, I will also check off a few small tasks.

Set Time Limits

For those who struggle to work within the bounds of objective time, setting time limits on your work can help. If you have been putting off a project, dreading the work or the amount of time it will take, tell yourself you only have to work on it for fifteen minutes. Set the timer and start.

That fifteen minutes will pass quickly, and you may feel motivated to keep going. But rather than continue, honor your internal commitment to stop. This does two things. First, it will give you a sense of healthy control over your work. Second, it will help train your brain to get a better sense of the passage of time.

Time limits also motivate us to work more efficiently and quickly. It can even be a game when we try this approach on certain jobs. Set the timer for fifteen minutes and see how quickly you can clean your desk at the end of the day, or see how much the kids can pick up around the house.

Procrastinators often misjudge the amount of time things take to accomplish. As you set time limits, you'll learn how much time tasks really take. You might put off cleaning your bathroom, thinking it will take hours, when in fact you can do a good job in thirty minutes.

Try this approach multiple times throughout the day on different tasks. You'll soon increase your confidence in your sense of time and find yourself moving forward on projects you've been resisting.

Value Small Pockets of Time

Sometimes I talk myself out of starting a project because I only have a short block of time. Some work does require sustained focus, but not all work. I don't need an hour to set an appointment, make an airline reservation, or order something online.

When setting a plan for the day or week, add a few small tasks to your list. Then, when a little window of time opens up, you can quickly check one more item off your list.

Valuing minutes, not just hours, helps us become wise time managers. I often think of the parable of the talents, with its three servants who were entrusted with three different amounts of money while their master went on a trip. Two of the servants invested their "talents" and got a return. But the servant who only had one talent buried it in the ground, receiving harsh consequences when his master returned.

Did the servant not value his one talent? Did he think it insignificant compared to what other servants received? The Lord values what seems meager to others. Every effort we make, every small step we take, if it is done with a right heart, pleases God.

Zechariah 4:10 says, "Do not despise these small beginnings, for the LORD rejoices to see the work begin" (NLT).

Perhaps the wisest thing we can do is to learn to value our minutes. The greatest accomplishments on earth started with someone working for sixty seconds.

Reevaluate the Value of Your Time

One of the time wasters listed earlier was tasks you could have delegated. For a mom, this might be when you fold the clothes instead of teaching your children to do it. For a busy home manager, perhaps hiring someone to mow the lawn is a better choice than doing it yourself.

As we become better time managers, we must consider the value of our time and when it's better to delegate a task. Marketing guru Seth Godin writes:

> One of the milestones every entrepreneur passes is when she stops thinking of people she hires as expensive ("I could do that job for free") and starts thinking of them as cheap ("This frees me up to do something more profitable").
>
> When you get rid of every job you do that could be done by someone else, something needs to fill your time. And what you discover is that you're imagining growth, building partnerships, rethinking the enterprise (working on your business instead of in it, as the emyth guys would say). Right now, you don't even see those jobs, because you're busy doing things that feel efficient instead.[4]

When I consider my priorities and the best use of my time, one of the questions I ask myself is, *What can only I do?* I mentioned this in chapter 3, but it bears repeating.

There are really only a few things that *only* I can do. No one else can nurture my personal faith in God. Only I can do that. No one else can get my body to the gym or limit my sugar intake. I have the final decision on those responsibilities.

The same applies to my marriage and children. I am the only woman who is my husband's wife. Unless I want to abdicate that role, it is up to me to become the best wife I can be. And God has given me five children to mother. Just about everything else in my life could be done by someone else.

If I want to make the most of my time, I need to release responsibility. Not every task, volunteer position, responsibility at work, or job around the house is my responsibility.

This is harder than it sounds. Many procrastinators are also perfectionists, so letting go of setting the Thanksgiving table might feel impossible. Letting older children iron their own clothes might send shivers down your spine. But what is your time worth? Is it worth a task being done differently than you would do it?

Another reason it might be hard to delegate is procrastinators often feel unworthy of help. They are ashamed of their procrastination and feel like they should be able to do it all. I understand this feeling. But the more I'm learning to delegate, the more confident I'm becoming in what I do well. Plus I'm learning to trust others to a greater degree.

Delegating is a skill we all can learn. There might be time spent training, but it will be worth it when you can fully release a responsibility. Plus, it's really a blessing to let others know we trust them. By delegating work, we build others up as well as free ourselves up.

If you don't have children around or the money to hire a professional, consider bartering skills with a friend. Perhaps you could make a few dinners in exchange for her running your errands. You also might find a teenager who's willing to work cheap.

The only reason to manage time wisely is so you can spend it on what matters most. That's not always work. Please make sure you end this chapter with that understanding. Sometimes the very best use of our time is to stop our work and snuggle up next to a loved one. Or sit by the bedside of a sick friend. Or walk in the park and pray. Or turn up the music and dance.

● PRACTICAL APPLICATION

We all wish we were better time managers. The good news is we all have the ability to make time for what matters most.

You've identified two areas of your life you want to master—one regular task and one personal goal. How can you better use the time you have right now to get started? Do you need to eliminate some time wasters? Schedule uninterrupted time? Preplan your week? What will you do differently with time in these two areas?

My regular task:

My personal goal:

13

Organizing Our Work

Sometimes our reasons for procrastination are complex. Fear is downright complicated and perfectionism is deeply rooted. It takes a lot of introspection to address those issues.

But the problem isn't always internal. Sometimes our procrastination is simply solved by changing our approach to two things:

1. How we organize our work
2. How we identify our work

Basically, a single to-do list is ineffective in managing our busy, multifaceted lives. We used to be able to compartmentalize work, home, church, and volunteer work—but that's just not possible now. We live integrated, interconnected lives. So how we *organize* our work needs to change.

Next, we should consider how we *identify* the work we need to do. Rather than vague goals, we can put things into concrete, specific statements, which takes our work from ethereal to real.

Sometimes, how we've identified and organized our workload has actually encouraged procrastination, but we can make changes that make a drastic difference—immediately. And it starts with trading in our traditional to-do list for a project management system.

A Project Management Approach

For years, I lived with an ongoing sense that I *should* be doing something at all times. It ate at me. Even when I was working on something important, there was a latent unease about what *else* I should be doing. It was a constant underlying stress even when there was no imminent deadline or threat.

It wasn't until I read David Allen's *Getting Things Done* that I discovered the reason why. Allen writes:

> The big problem is that your mind keeps reminding you of things when you can't do anything about them. It has no sense of past or future. That means that as soon as you tell yourself that you need to do something, and store it in your RAM (your mind), there's a part of you that thinks you should be doing that something all the time.[1]

Aha! That was it! There were so many things I knew I should be doing, so many vague goals and big ideas, that my mind felt overwhelmed by it all. Then, because there was so much to do, I just felt frozen much of the time.

When I feel overwhelmed, my gut reaction is to do one of two things. Either I jump into the fray and try to put out fires, feeling like a juggler at a fair with flaming torches. Or I shut down and can't do anything.

The solution, according to Allen, is to capture all those ideas, projects, dreams, goals, and tasks you know you need to do somewhere "safe." That way, you can tell your worried little mind to relax and enjoy the moment and not stress about what you'll forget.

That sounded so logical to me. Sure, I'd tried and failed to organize my workload like that so many times before. But as I continued to read Allen's book, I realized why my plans hadn't worked in the past. Before, I'd tried to put everything on *one* to-do list. Just one.

The problem with having one list is it's like trying to force a semitruck to drive down a country lane next to a bicycle. Or force my size 9 feet into dainty size 6 shoes. Some things just don't fit. Here's an example of what my list used to look like:

1. Make orthodontist appointment for Robbie
2. Plan Dylan's birthday party
3. Deposit check
4. Redesign blog
5. Buy dog food
6. Organize bedroom

These are all normal things a woman might do. So what was the problem?

The problem is three of those items aren't simple tasks. Calling the orthodontist's office takes one step, and it's done. Boom. Check that baby off the list!

But planning a party, redesigning a blog, and organizing a bedroom are made up of multiple tasks. To put them on a to-do list is just asking for failure . . . and a reason to procrastinate.

I'd look at my list, see "Clean the house," and feel discouraged before starting. And the procrastinator in me rose up and convinced me I didn't have time to tackle that—and anyway, where would I start? So I put that job to the bottom of my list, checked off everything else but that, and transferred it to the next list.

Here's what I've learned: cleaning the house isn't a task. It's a project. Projects don't belong on a to-do list. Only single-step tasks belong there.

Once I realized the mistake I'd been making for *years*, I realized I needed to toss my to-do list and start fresh.

Then I did something brave. I did a complete inventory of everything I needed to do. It took days to complete. I decided to include immediate needs and everything I'd been putting off. The small and the big all got listed.

Once I was sure I'd captured everything, I sat down and had a good cry. My life was seriously out of control.

No wonder I was procrastinating. There was no way I could get everything done in a timely fashion. To survive meant shuffling my priorities hourly.

Drying my tears, I reviewed the monstrous list and divided it into two categories: one-step tasks and multistep projects. That was better. But I wasn't done yet. I looked at all the projects and realized some of them were urgent and others weren't. So I divided that list into current and future projects.

There was one more step. Since every big project is completed one step at a time, I realized I needed to add tasks to each of my projects. So I got some more paper and started to list all the tasks I could think of for each project.

These lists became the foundation of my project management notebook. And yes, I did put it in a three-ring binder. I know I could have created a digital notebook, but there was something about putting it on paper that made it real for me. Although I still had a lot to do, having it all in one place brought relief.

Now writing my to-do list for the day is like going to a buffet and picking a piece of chicken here and a scoop of mac and cheese there. I look over my master lists and only put on my to-do list the tasks I can realistically accomplish that day. I might pick a simple task, like make an appointment, then pull another task from a project list.

This system revolutionized my approach to getting work done. It also eliminated a few of my reasons for procrastination, which

Included forgetting things (now they were in my safe place) and feeling overwhelmed when I looked at a big project on my to-do list.

Now my to-do list might have five items on it, rather than twenty-five. Five is much more manageable. And when I finish those five, I can go back for more from my project management list.

Over the years, this system has actually helped me manage my workload so well that I don't have to create massive master lists anymore. The process helped me realize I'd taken on too much, and I did some serious editing. But when I get overloaded—and it still does happen—I know to go back and create that master list again.

Breaking Down a Project into Tasks

Let's look at a hypothetical situation. Let's say you can't find your living room because it's cluttered with stacks of newspapers, magazines, DVDs, kids' toys, clothes, and so on. If I told you, in the midst of your chaos, "Go organize your living room!" you would laugh in my face. And I would deserve it. Because we both know you would have done it if you could.

But what if I suggested you gather all the old newspapers and put them in a cardboard box? You could manage that. Then if I said go gather up all the DVDs and put them in a wicker basket, you could do that.

Tackling a big project takes the same approach. We break down a big task into little tasks that are logical to us. We do this type of strategizing in real life all the time. If we want to plan a vacation, we need to arrange a flight or driving plan, a place to stay, activities, and meals. The bigger the vacation, the more detailed the planning.

This is no different. No one can just "get organized" without some kind of plan. What that plan looks like is completely up to you.

When you're facing a big project that feels overwhelming, it helps to identify little tasks that will move the project toward completion. The very act of listing the steps is motivating. My friend Kathi Lipp, coauthor of *The Cure for the "Perfect" Life*, writes about the power of identifying tasks in a project:

> I spent a month having the same item on my to-do list—and it was only a fifteen minute project: Write fifteen minutes on chapter four. Simple enough, right? So why did I spend weeks avoiding it?
>
> Because it felt really big. I knew I needed to go through some files to actually find chapter four, and when I finally found it, I didn't remember what was already written. Would I be pleasantly surprised on how much work I'd already accomplished? Probably not. My mind turned to fear and doom and the looming task.
>
> What I had here was really two tasks: 1. Find and open the file. 2. Write for fifteen minutes. Once I realized it was two tasks, it felt doable—like I was getting a check mark for each of the things I was actually doing.[2]

If breaking down a project feels impossible, try brainstorming. Don't worry about the order these tasks need to be accomplished in, just start writing thoughts down as they come to you.

For example, I took my mother on a special vacation, just the two of us, and planning for it felt overwhelming. My husband normally does the vacation planning in our household, so it was out of my comfort zone to handle all the details. I wasn't sure what to do first. Did I reserve the plane tickets or the hotels?

Maybe that sounds silly to you vacation planners, but it overwhelmed me. This trip sat on my project list for months until I finally broke it down into tasks. Here's what it looked like.

- Set dates for trip
- Make airline reservations
- Reserve car
- Identify city and state stops for each day (we traveled from Charleston, South Carolina, to New Orleans)

- Research and reserve hotels in each city
- Research and list tourist options in each city
- List restaurant options in each city

Once I had the tasks identified, I was able to get them done. And my mother and I had a great trip.

What projects are you struggling to start? Take some time to write out some of the steps needed. If you are a perfectionist and the thought of making a mistake on your list worries you, try these approaches:

- Write all the steps on sticky notes and put them on a wall
- Write the steps on a whiteboard, so you can easily erase
- Draw a circle with your project name in the middle and spokes radiating from the circle with different tasks listed

This process can be done with every project you have—whether it takes two steps or two hundred. Once you've identified the assortment of tasks needed, you can pick one to put on your very manageable to-do list. And when you've gotten that done, you can pick another.

And very soon you'll find yourself accomplishing big projects that you never thought you would.

Be Specific in Your Direction

A project management approach is how I *organize* my work, but I've also had to change how I *identify* my work. Turns out that language really makes a difference in whether I procrastinate or address my work.

Have you ever told a child to go clean up his room only to walk in later and find him sitting on the floor playing with Legos?

I knew better than to send my children off without very specific, limited instructions. But in my haste, rather than taking time to clearly list the tasks needed to return order to a room, I'd just spout off a go-clean-your-room command.

Those types of direction were so vague my three boys found them nearly impossible to follow. When we adopted our daughters, I wanted to believe they would think more like me. Maybe I secretly hoped we shared some special female tidy-gene since we didn't share DNA. So I tried the same vague directions one day and sent them to clean up their room.

An hour later I walked in to find clothes and toys strewn everywhere! Under-the-bed boxes on top of the beds, dresser drawers open with nightgowns and T-shirts spilling out, and all the clothes from the closet on the floor rather than hanging on the rod. When I asked what they were doing, my youngest (age nine) smiled and replied, "Organizing!"

Ahem. Apparently there was a common denominator with the miscommunication problem, and it was me.

We've come a long way since then, and I've realized that very few people have the natural ability to take a big assignment and break it down into manageable tasks. Which is why so many goals and resolutions are left on the front page of spiral notebooks, never to be checked off.

The more vague the goal, the less likely it will be achieved.

The problem wasn't just my directions to my children. I also announced those vague types of goals to myself. Perhaps you've also said something like this to yourself before: *Someday, I'm going to get this house organized.* Or, *One of these days, I'm going to take some time for myself.*

I love those statements. We should all get our homes organized and make time for ourselves. But those are too abstract to be reachable goals. There are no edges, no beginning or end. "Someday" and "one of these days" aren't on any calendar I've ever seen. And how would I know when to put a check mark in front of it?

If we want to move forward in accomplishing our best work, we need to identify an abstract thought and turn it into a concrete statement.

It's Hard to Reach a Vague Goal

Procrastinators have a habit of setting vague goals. It's easy to say things like:

I'm going to get better at remembering my friends' birthdays.

I'm going to start eating healthy.

I'm going to keep my house clutter-free.

I'm going to save money.

But no amount of wishing, hoping, or dreaming things are going to be different *this time* will accomplish vague goals. Without specifics, they're just nice ideas that bring feelings of guilt when we think about them. They're slippery and hard to grab hold of.

It seems I'm always learning this lesson. And it happened yet again when I recently decided to go back to the gym to lift weights. I've lifted weights before, but always in a class or with a trainer, someone who designed a plan for me. This time, I reasoned, I could do it on my own with no written directions. So I filled my water bottle, grabbed a hand towel to cover the sweaty weight benches, and headed to the gym.

My heart was in the right place, but my feet just wandered. I did a few leg presses, then staggered over to the chest press machine. The weights felt so heavy after my exercise sabbatical that I abandoned my lifting plans and turned to my go-to workout: the elliptical machine.

A few days later I tried the weight-lifting idea again. I remembered that when I'd worked out before, the trainer had varied the muscle groups each time. So I did a little triceps work, then some biceps work. Then a few halfhearted lunges. By then I was having trouble catching my breath and decided it would be safer to just get on the elliptical again.

My dreams of getting stronger and more toned were evaporating. I had lots of enthusiasm but no planning. And without specifics, I reverted to my old habits.

The idea of lifting weights is a nice wish. But it's not specific. If I walked into the gym and lifted one weight, would I have accomplished my goal? Of course not. I knew I needed a specific plan, but I procrastinated.

The hard truth was, that vague goal was safer for me. It had absolutely no measurable actions. And with no measurable actions, I couldn't fail.

Is this sounding familiar? If at this point you need to go back and reread the chapters on fear and perfectionism, feel free to return. I'll be here when you get back.

I've set too many "goals" that have no boundaries. There's no way to know when I've met them. A serious goal has structure. It's specific. It can be measured. Someone else can see me do it.

So many times we neglect to add structure to our great ideas. Maybe it's because we don't want to be held accountable. Or maybe it's because we can't figure out how to dissect our big ideas into tasks we can actually accomplish.

So our hopes and wishes and big ideas just float somewhere in the nether regions of our minds, popping in and out of consciousness—usually when we can't do anything about them. If we want to get serious about addressing those things we've put off, we must lasso those vagaries and tie them down with specifics.

Setting Measurable Goals

In order for us to tackle our procrastination, we must start by being very clear with ourselves. Giving my children unclear directions is unfair to them. And it's unfair to do that to myself.

The more we can define our expectations, the more likely we are to achieve them. For instance, let's say I want to send out Christmas cards this year. It's been a few years since I've done it, and this year I really want to connect on paper with the people I love.

The first step is to write this down as a project. I could write "Send Christmas cards." But to make this goal measurable, I need to add specifics. So an alternative way to write this is "Mail Christmas cards by December 10." That gives me a deadline that already increases the urgency.

Here are some examples of concrete goals:

- Save five hundred dollars by December 31
- Clean the bathroom by Tuesday
- Read chapters 2 and 3 by ten o'clock Thursday morning
- Get up daily at 6:30 a.m. and read one chapter of the Bible
- Work on a sewing project two hours every Saturday

These specifics also need to be realistic. If it's December 8 when I write the goal to send out Christmas cards on the 10th, it's probably not going to happen.

Specific details keep tasks and projects from being slippery. And they make me honest with myself. If I'm not willing to be specific, I'm not really interested in doing the work.

The more specific my goals, the more doable they are. The next question is, do I share them on Facebook?

The Difference between Boasting and Setting Goals

One of the dangers I've found in setting goals is sharing them with others. Did you know that making your goal public could backfire?

I sure do. I once announced on my blog I was going to lose weight—and gained five pounds. Announcing your goals isn't the same as having an accountability partner. This is where we procrastinators get mixed up. We think just sharing our intent with someone will motivate us to get it done. However, that's not the truth.

It's dangerously satisfying to set goals. According to several scientific studies, it seems some of us get enough mental gratification just by talking about our goals that we skip actually doing the work.

There have been times when I've taken pride in myself for identifying a worthwhile goal. It's like there's this striving little part of me that puffs up ever so slightly when declaring what I'm *going* to accomplish. It's definitely a cousin of boasting, only so much more refined. Do I just imagine you admire me when I speak of my goals? Do they make me seem more intellectual or bolder than I am?

The Bible is quite clear that actions speak louder than words.

There's an interesting proverb found in 1 Kings that rings true. It's spoken by Ahab, king of Israel, when he faced attack by Ben-Hadad, the king of Aram. Ben-Hadad sent threatening messages, trying to intimidate Ahab. But Ahab wouldn't be shaken. In the face of the final threat, Ahab says to Beh-Hadad's messenger, "Tell him: 'One who puts on his armor should not boast like one who takes it off'" (1 Kings 20:11).

I can get so excited about my goals, especially when I've finally decided to tackle them, that I want to share them with friends. But unless I've entered into an accountability relationship with someone, it's better to keep my goals between me and God.

● PRACTICAL APPLICATION

Without a specific plan, it's easy for our highest and best goals to never be more than vague ideas. In this chapter we discussed the positive impact of properly organizing and identifying our work. We also discussed setting measurable goals.

Apply what you've learned in this chapter to your two challenge areas. Set a measurable goal for your regular task, and break down your personal goal into steps.

My regular task:

My personal goal:

14

Small Changes Matter

Productive people know that it's often the small changes we make in our days that produce the greatest amount of impact. This is especially true when dealing with tasks that we'd really rather not do.

Procrastinators often repeat the same habits, hoping for different results. We believe the solution is for us to just try harder. But that's not always the case. Sometimes we need a small tweak in our approach to find success. Facing our procrastination takes creativity, persistence, and a willingness to try something new.

There are some changes you can make that will help you battle the urge to procrastinate. They might seem simple, but sometimes simple is best.

Prioritize Life-Giving Activities

When I've asked women what they tend to put off, a common thread surfaced. Women often procrastinate that which fuels their hearts, minds, and souls.

Here's a truth to hold on to: you are not a machine!

You cannot run nonstop, 24/7, pushing yourself to exhaustion, using caffeine as your energy source, and caring for everyone else's needs forever. You will implode.

When we try to do this, we become worn-out, burned-out, broken-down versions of ourselves with nothing left to give anyone.

This happened to me one year, and it took me by surprise. I knew I was getting stressed, and deadlines were coming faster than I could meet them. My time with the Lord had diminished, and I'd stopped doing anything for myself. I was on automatic go-mode.

Then someone at work crossed a line. At least that's how I saw it. They made a decision in an area that was my responsibility, and rather than thinking the best about them or making a phone call to discuss the decision, I shot off an angry email, copying a few other people on it. My email absolutely devastated this person, who felt blindsided by my reaction.

We worked through it and both of us apologized, but I was shocked and surprised by my actions. I'm not typically reactive, nor do I tend to think the worst of people. In fact, I'm very thick-skinned and not easily offended. What happened to me? Why had I overreacted in such an unloving way?

It took time to process the situation, but the Lord didn't let me let it go. Over and over I thought about how I should have done something different. One day in the car, out of the blue, an idea came to me: Could I have been burned-out?

I knew I'd been working more than ever. In fact, six months before my meltdown, my part-time assistant resigned and I'd assumed her job on top of my own. I thought I was handling things well . . . but apparently I wasn't.

Walking into the house, I rushed to my computer, typed "burn-out" in the search bar, and brought up list after list describing my heart:

- Cynical or critical of others
- Irritable or impatient
- Feelings of detachment or apathy
- Lack of interest in things that used to interest you
- Lack of energy to be productive

Burnout had crept up on me until it exploded onto a friend. Looking back, I'd definitely seen the signs but hadn't put them together and given them a name. Once I did, I was able to immediately make changes.

I had to guard time for myself. And getting back into praying and reading my Bible every day was the number one change. I purchased a little spiral notebook so I could record my daily reading and write a prayer request. Just having a record of my time with the Lord helped me feel better.

I told my husband, and he and I made plans to have a date night every few weeks. He knows I love music and the arts, so he researched local plays and musical performances and penciled in dates for the next six months.

I also love to be with my children. And my three oldest had moved out, which was very hard on me. So I became more intentional in spending time with them.

My heart was running on empty and it needed to be refilled.

Rather than just taking on the extra work, I should have told someone how overworked I was. Because I telecommute, no one could really know unless I spoke up. I soon got a new assistant, and within a few months I was feeling more like myself.

What brings you joy? What is life-giving to you? Take some time to make a list of the things you love to do. Then schedule one thing a week for the next month.

Once your heart is healthy, you will feel braver about facing unpleasant tasks in a timely manner.

Build Renewal into Your Week

My burnout experience happened because I had neglected to care for myself. If we want to sustain energy to fulfill God's calling on our lives and complete the work He has given us to do, we should build renewal into our lives on a weekly basis. Waiting until we fall apart creates lots of collateral damage.

God actually designed the need for rest and renewal into our minds and bodies. Obviously we need sleep, but God also designed us to need rest at other times.

As we become more aware of our body's ultradian rhythm, we can plan difficult tasks for when our energy levels are highest. Then, as our stamina diminishes, we can undertake less demanding work.

We tend to ignore those lulls in energy and instead try to sustain a high level of focus by pushing through, perhaps with coffee. Rather than ignore these lulls, however, try working with them. When you feel your energy level drop, take a break. Allow your mind and your body to relax like it wants to do. After ten or fifteen minutes, start back on your work. Consider it an organic approach.

The other renewal God has designed is the Sabbath. In fact, resting one day a week was so important to God that He incorporated it into the Ten Commandments given to Moses and the Israelites.

Exodus 20 records the commandments, and the fourth one reads: "Remember the Sabbath day by keeping it holy. Six days you shall labor and do all your work, but the seventh day is a sabbath to the LORD your God. On it you shall not do any work" (Exod. 20:8–10).

The Sabbath wasn't just a good idea. It was a sign of the promise made between God and His people. In Exodus 31:12–13, God spoke to Moses, "Say to the Israelites, 'You must observe my Sabbaths. This will be a sign between me and you for the generations to come, so you may know that I am the Lord, who makes you holy.'"

So many times, I said to my children, "Trust me. I know you want to do XYZ, but it's not wise. Please trust that I know what's best." I saw dangers and anticipated consequences they couldn't. And oh, how it hurt my heart when they didn't listen to me.

Now compare my puny human wisdom with God's perfect wisdom—my feeble attempts at anticipating consequences with His omniscience. And explain why any of us would ignore God's request to honor the Sabbath. Why do we think we know better than God?

I stumble and fall more times than I succeed in this commandment. I tend to fudge the definition of "work" and justify whatever task I'm doing. But this commandment isn't just to not work. It's to rest.

I'm committed to trusting God in a greater way with the Sabbath. And I'm trusting that after a true day of rest, I'll be refreshed and refueled to pick back up the next day with increased effectiveness.

Develop Smart Routines

Routines are powerful tools to get things done. In chapter 11, I shared how decision making reduces our willpower, and that routines can help reduce decisions. And in chapter 10, I discussed how habits are formed and how we can replace bad ones with good.

As you think about routines, consider times of the day when you could develop a simple routine. Not only do they reduce decisions and establish good habits but routines can also drastically reduce the stress in your life. This is especially true if you have children, who tend to thrive with simple routines.

When trying a new routine, writing it out can be helpful. I've done this many times with my children and actually posted the routine somewhere visible.

When we first adopted our daughters, they wanted to eat all the time. They didn't understand the feeling of being full—they only knew hunger. So after consulting with a dietician, I learned I had to teach them there were times to eat and times to not eat. Even though my heart wanted to give them food all the time, it wasn't healthy for them. So I wrote out a schedule for the day with times for meals and frequent small snacks. They couldn't read yet, so I used it as a teaching tool. And they learned the daily meal routine very quickly. Here are some suggestions for helpful routines for your day.

Starting Work

Most of us head straight to email. But what if you didn't? What if you started your day by tackling your most important task for the first sixty to ninety minutes? This routine could dramatically alter the rest of your day.

After School

If you have school-age children at home, set an order for whatever is important for your child, such as rest, snacks, chores, homework, reading, and play. Be faithful to that routine until your child can't imagine not doing homework before playtime.

After Work

Do you tend to come home and collapse on the couch, never touch housework, and run out for fast food? What routine can you establish? Maybe hang your keys on their hook, put away your purse, sort and file the mail, start dinner, do five minutes of pickup, and do five minutes of cleaning.

After Dinner

Are dishes left on the counter? What if your routine consisted of completely cleaning the kitchen before any other evening activities?

Before Bed

Before turning out the lights, could you read your Bible for ten minutes, review your to-do list for the next day, straighten the living room, and gather up any papers or books that need to leave the house with you in the morning?

As I shared earlier, establishing a morning routine with a timed schedule changed my family's mornings from chaotic to peaceful. Which also meant I wasn't wasting valuable energy and willpower trying to get kids motivated and out the door on time.

Pick any problem area of your day and consider if a routine might help.

Take Time to Daydream

Henry Ford said, "Thinking is the hardest work there is, which is probably the reason so few engage in it."[1]

Are you procrastinating on a project that seems too complicated? Perhaps you tried to work on it once and got nowhere. Maybe it's time to stop working and start daydreaming.

With technology literally at our fingertips all day, finding time to think is precious. We are switched on "go" most of the time, actively doing something.

And yet our minds are the greatest gift God has given us for managing our workload. The problem is we fill them with so much outside input that our internal creative resources are untapped.

There are times when analytical thinking is required to solve a problem. But sometimes we think we have to stay chained to the problem to find a solution when what we should do is stop the work and give our minds free rein to do what they were designed to do—search for creative solutions.

It is important to allow ourselves time to think. When our minds are relaxed, our thoughts drift. And as they drift, we see connections we missed when we were focused. For example, consider the invention of the Post-it note, which was a blending of a bookmark and weak glue. They are brilliant, and so useful they have become an "ubiquitous fixture of stationery cupboards worldwide."[2] And that idea happened in a church, not a lab.

Reward Yourself

All parents understand the power of rewards. Whether it's stickers on a chore chart, a hug, positive words, or a trip to McDonald's for extra effort in school, children respond to positive rewards.

I wonder if we think we've outgrown the need for rewards. Do they seem childish, perhaps?

God doesn't think so.

There are over eighty verses in the Bible that refer to rewards. From Genesis 15:1, where God says to Abram, "Do not be afraid, Abram. I am your shield, your very great reward," to Jesus's words in Matthew 5:46, "If you love those who love you, what reward will you get? Are not even the tax collectors doing that?" and on to the last book of the Bible and the Lord's promise in Revelation 22:12, "Look, I am coming soon! My reward is with me, and I will give to each person according to what they have done."

God created us to desire rewards. And in most biblical cases, we are rewarded for doing the right thing. So perhaps we need to stop feeling guilty for desiring some kind of reward and instead use them to motivate ourselves to overcome procrastination.

I'm guilty of assigning myself a reward only when I've completed my ultimate goal. But rather than inspiring me to action, a reward that far away actually demotivates me. This reinforces my perfectionist thinking that the only thing to be celebrated is the completed project.

What I should do is celebrate progress with small rewards along the way. Your first reward might be just for starting! And that's okay.

Make a list of small rewards that will motivate you to complete smaller steps but won't detract from your forward motion, such as five minutes on Facebook or a piece of chocolate candy. These will serve as a mental break as well as a reward.

Plan midsized rewards for completing project milestones. Perhaps these are ordering pizza for dinner or buying a new shirt. Then save the big reward for total completion of the project.

Procrastinators tend to be harsh on themselves, much harsher than others are. As we celebrate our progress, we are learning to treat ourselves kindly. Plus we are building in motivation to press on when we might rather quit. And that is a win-win in my book.

Call a Friend

One year, a friend called and asked if I wanted to share the expense of materials for making homemade gifts. Her idea was to buy mason jars and fill them with ingredients for cookies, then give them to friends and neighbors.

Since I'm not a very good shopper and tend to procrastinate on buying gifts, this sounded like a great idea to me. So we divvied up the shopping list of ingredients, met one Saturday, layered flour, brown sugar, and chocolate chips into jars, decorated them, and added crafty labels. And I checked ten people off my gift list.

If the gift giving had been up to me, I would have wandered about the mall, wasted hours, and ended up with something impersonal and cheap.

Tackling a dreaded task with a friend made it easy and fun. Plus I (and ten of my friends) benefited from her creativity and energy.

Procrastinators tend to think we're responsible for everything. We refuse to delegate, and we suffer for it. But by enlisting the help of a friend, we are still doing the work—and accomplishing more than we could alone.

Ecclesiastes 4:9–10 affirms this truth: "Two are better than one, because they have a good return for their labor: If either of them falls down, one can help the other up. But pity anyone who falls and has no one to help them up."

Friends can help each other clean, organize, and decorate. They can barter tasks, like trading ironing for mending. I've gotten together with friends to help me brainstorm a big project as I pick their brains for creative ideas.

And even when friends aren't physically helping us, just their presence can be motivating. I have friends who plan time to get together to work on their individual projects, like scrapbooking or crafting. For a few years, a friend and I met halfway between our cities for a writing retreat.

If no friend who'd be willing to help you immediately comes to mind, then offer to help someone else with their work. You might find that by offering to bless another, God will bless you.

Find an Accountability Partner

The Bible is clear we are to guard against a prideful heart, and boasting is a clear sign that something's not right. Proverbs 27:1 gives this wise warning: "Do not boast about tomorrow, for you do not know what a day may bring." And Proverbs 16:18 warns, "Pride goes before destruction, a haughty spirit before a fall."

As we address the issue of procrastination in our lives, it's good to have a humble heart. And one way we keep ourselves humble is to confess our weakness to another person and ask if we can be accountable to them with our progress. James 5:16 says, "Therefore confess your sins to each other and pray for each other so that you may be healed. The prayer of a righteous person is powerful and effective."

This verse can be confusing. But it's important to note that it doesn't say confess your sins to each other and you'll be *forgiven*. Only God through Christ can forgive us. But it says we "may be healed." I believe the key to this healing is humility. It's not easy to confess weakness to someone else. I'd much rather appear to have everything under control. But confessing sin and weakness breaks the hold pride has over me.

Weight is a constant struggle for me, and a few years ago my friend Karen and I agreed to be accountable to each other. We agreed to take a picture of the number on the scale one day a week and text it to each other. What a powerful motivator this was for me. Just knowing I would be honest with Karen helped me make better decisions.

Procrastination can be isolating. We're ashamed of our lack of self-control and the consequences of our choices. To make a connection with someone who passes no judgment can breathe hope into our hopelessness.

A key for finding an effective accountability partner is to pick someone who is both tender and tough. Both a prayer warrior and a cheerleader. And someone who needs your help as much as you need theirs. Finding an accountability partner helps us live out the Bible's command in Galatians 6:2 to "carry each other's burdens, and in this way you will fulfill the law of Christ."

● PRACTICAL APPLICATION

This chapter contained lots of tips for making small but important changes in how you approach your work. As you consider the two assignments you gave yourself at the beginning of the book, is there anything in this chapter that might help you face them more effectively? Does your personal exhaustion (physical, spiritual, and emotional) hinder you? Do you need to write a routine to incorporate your regular tasks? Do you need to spend time daydreaming or ask for help to tackle your personal goal? Write down some ideas to try.

My regular task:

My personal goal:

15

When Is It Not Procrastination?

As we reach the end of our time together, I want to reaffirm a message I shared at the beginning: all procrastination is delay, but not all delay is procrastination. We can be hard enough on ourselves without assuming unnecessary guilt. So I wanted to share a few examples of delay that is not procrastination.

Sometimes the right thing is to reschedule, reevaluate, or change our plans. Sometimes we have to abandon preset goals for a greater goal. Other times God has us do a 180-degree turn, and it would be disobedient to keep going the same direction. Sometimes God gives us a blessing, or allows a challenge, that requires us to postpone our plans.

A wise woman listens and watches to see what God might be doing. And she adapts her plans to His when necessary.

As you consider your assignments, job, responsibilities, and priorities, consider if perhaps the right thing is to address them later. Let's look at three situations when the right decision is to delay.

One: When It's Smart Planning

My sister Paula told me she procrastinates on mail. So I asked her why. She explained that her days as an elementary schoolteacher are *filled* with things she has to do, like lessons to write and papers to grade, and when she gets home the last thing she wants to do is sort through mail. Also, because her husband is legally blind, not only does she have to review her mail but process his as well.

I nodded my head in understanding. I knew this school year was particularly difficult; her reasons made complete sense. Then she explained that on Saturdays, she sits down with the stack of mail and sorts through it. She felt so guilty because she believed she ought to be sorting through it every day.

I smiled at my sister and said, "That's not procrastination. That's smart time management!"

My sister intentionally postponed a task until she had the mental space to deal with it. It wasn't an indefinite delay, only a few days.

Her delay was wise. She knew her energy was compromised and her attitude might not be chirpy. It was better to put off the task of opening the mail until she was ready to deal with it.

Sometimes we go through difficult days, weeks, or seasons of life when we don't handle challenges with the same gusto. If it's been one of "those" days, it's better to try again another day.

The reason for delay might also be financial. You might feel like it's procrastination, but when proceeding with the work would put you into debt unnecessarily, then it's best to reschedule the task until you can afford it.

We must be honest with ourselves, however, if these types of situations seem to happen more often than not. Patterns of delay are likely procrastination.

Two: When Priorities Change

Sometimes our lives change drastically but we refuse to accept the change. We soldier on as if nothing has changed and get further and further behind. We believe we *should* be able to manage it all because we used to before the change happened. This happened to me after my first three children were born.

Joshua Owen Whitwer changed the world as I knew it . . . forever. But at first, I didn't accept the changes. I adored my little son and loved him more than I thought possible. But I never considered changing my life plans for him. After a short maternity break, I returned to work.

Twenty-six months later Dylan was born, and twenty-one months after that, Robbie joined the family. When Robbie was born, Joshua was still three. And I was a mess.

The next three years were the hardest of my life. Frustration reigned in my heart and mind as I tried to regain my "old life." It was like trying to walk against the current . . . in mud to my knees . . . carrying three children in my arms. Let's just say it wasn't graceful.

Although I did cut my work hours back some, I tried to keep the same pace with everything else. I kept all my volunteer leadership roles at church and maintained my commitments to small groups and studies.

Only God didn't give me three little boys who were content to sit and play quietly while Mommy went to a meeting. My three blessings were physically active as soon as they could crawl. They wanted to run, jump, climb, sword fight, and do everything with great enthusiasm. We did nothing quietly and started calling ourselves the Loud Family.

I might have continued on my path of insisting on having it all and doing it all—at great cost to my sanity and my children—had God not intervened in a huge way. I'm convinced God orchestrated a job loss for my husband and a move across the country for our family to get me to reevaluate my choices.

I realized I had to let go of all I was hanging on to in order to accept the new assignment God had given me. I had to postpone personal goals and dreams in order to embrace the new goals and dreams God had given me.

By 2005, when we adopted our two daughters, I had learned this lesson. I again put off personal goals and dreams to be available to my children. I thought it would be for just three years, but it turned into closer to ten.

This wasn't the plan I had for myself. I wanted to achieve more by a younger age. But God's plan for me involved two little girls who needed a mother who was physically and emotionally present. He knew it wasn't going to be an easy road for our family.

When God changes our circumstances, we should consider changing our priorities. Otherwise we will have unrealistic expectations and put undue pressure on ourselves and our loved ones. When priorities change, we can renegotiate the contract we have with ourselves and postpone certain work and responsibilities.

Three: When We Are Waiting on God

Finally, sometimes, for no apparent reason, God says *wait*. It would be nice if His voice were audible; that would be easy to identify. But most of the time it's not that obvious.

God's yield sign often looks like a dead end as you pursue your goals. It might be a closed door of opportunity, like a *no* from an employer or a house that just won't sell no matter what you do.

It's not easy to know if you should try again or try a different approach. For me, God's "wait" is clear only after I've tried my hardest and come to the end of my resources. I tend to be a little more "full steam ahead" than contemplative. Then when I've finally surrendered, I see God's hand has been holding back the answer or goal.

Although I don't like to wait, God always has a plan to work things out for my good. So I must trust His "wait" is either to protect me or to prepare me for what's ahead.

One Final Thought

Thank you for taking this journey with me. Facing procrastination isn't easy. You're very brave to face an area of your life that needs to be strengthened. Always remember that procrastination doesn't define you. Your worth and value will never be found in how quickly you complete a task or how many items you check off your to-do list.

Once you identify the reasons for your procrastination, you can start replacing lies with truth and implementing smart strategies into your days. Then one day you'll realize fear has no hold on you and perfectionism doesn't threaten to put you in a chokehold as you face your best, most creative, most challenging work with a smile.

And on that day, please let me know so I can celebrate with you! It would be my honor.

● PERSONAL APPLICATION

You made it! You finished this book, and that is cause for celebration. But I know your true satisfaction will be when you see areas of your life change. And they will. You aren't destined to be haunted by undone tasks and ignored dreams. You are empowered and equipped by God to complete every task and assignment that is yours to complete.

Let's take a final look at the two areas you wanted to change. Perhaps you have actually checked them off your to-do list already. If that's the case, what will you address next? If not, what do you need to change in order to celebrate your completion of this work?

Wherever you are in the process, know I'm standing on the sidelines cheering you on. You can do it!

My regular task:

My personal goal:

Notes

Chapter 2 What Is Procrastination?

1. Jane B. Burka, PhD, and Lenora M. Yuen, PhD, *Procrastination: Why You Do It, What to Do About It NOW* (Cambridge, MA: DaCapo Press, 1983, 2008), 9.

2. Ibid., 10.

Chapter 3 Understanding Some of the Whys

1. As quoted in Christopher McDougall, *Born to Run* (New York: Alfred A. Knopf, 2009), 175–76.

2. Lysa TerKeurst, *The Best Yes* (Nashville: Nelson, 2014), 155.

Chapter 4 Assessing the Price We Pay

1. Liberty Savard, *Shattering Your Strongholds* (Gainesville, FL: Bridge-Logos Publishers, 1992), 27.

2. "Mammography: Benefits, Risks, What You Need to Know," BreastCancer.org, accessed March 23, 2015, http://www.breastcancer.org/symptoms/testing/types/mammograms/benefits_risks.

3. "Chronic Stress Puts Your Health at Risk," The Mayo Clinic, July 11, 2013, http://www.mayoclinic.org/healthy-living/stress-management/in-depth/stress/art-20046037.

Chapter 5 Myth Busters

1. Berit Brogaard, "What Happens During an Adrenaline Rush?" Livestrong.com, August 16, 2013, http://www.livestrong.com/article/203790-what-happens-during-an-adrenaline-rush/.

2. Amy Arnsten, Carolyn M. Mazure, and Rajita Sinha, "Everyday Stress Can Shut Down the Brain's Chief Command Center," *Scientific American*, April 9, 2012.

3. Brian Tracy, *Eat That Frog!* (San Francisco: Berrett-Koehler, 2007), 30.

4. Timothy A. Pychyl, *Solving the Procrastination Puzzle* (New York: Penguin, 2013), 31.

5. Josh James Riebock, *Heroes and Monsters: An Honest Look at the Struggle within All of Us* (Grand Rapids: Baker Books, 2012), 166–67.

Chapter 6 Overcoming Our Fears

1. Burka and Yuen, *Procrastination*, 92.

2. Gerald Beals, "Thomas Edison 'Quotes,'" *Thomas Alva Edison Quotes*, accessed March 23, 2015, http://www.thomasedison.com/quotes.html.

Chapter 7 Too Busy?

1. Tim Kreider, "The 'Busy' Trap," *New York Times*, June 30, 2012, http://opinionator.blogs.nytimes.com/2012/06/30/the-busy-trap/?_r=0.

2. Carol Brazo, *No Ordinary Home: The Uncommon Art of Christ-centered Homemaking* (Sisters, OR: Multnomah, 1995), 24.

3. "John D. Rockefeller," *New World Encyclopedia*, accessed March 23, 2015, http://www.newworldencyclopedia.org/entry/John_D._Rockefeller.

4. "Johann Wolfgang von Goethe Quotes," Goodreads.com, accessed March 23, 2015, http://www.goodreads.com/quotes/2326-things-which-matter-most-must-never-be-at-the-mercy.

Chapter 8 Thinking with Focus and Clarity

1. "Starving for Sleep: America's Hunger Games," The Better Sleep Council, February 2014, http://bettersleep.org/better-sleep/the-science-of-sleep/sleep-statistics-research/starving-for-sleep-americas-hunger-games/.

2. "Brain May Flush Out Toxins During Sleep," National Institutes of Health, October 17, 2013, http://www.nih.gov/news/health/oct2013/ninds-17.htm.

3. Daniel J. Levitin, "Hit the Reset Button in Your Brain," *New York Times*, August 9, 2014.

4. Gary Griffiths, "The Web Is Much Bigger (And Smaller) Than You Think," *Forbes*, April 24, 2012, http://www.forbes.com/sites/ciocentral/2012/04/24/the-web-is-much-bigger-and-smaller-than-you-think/.

5. "Brain Basics: Know Your Brain," National Institute of Neurological Disorders and Strokes, April 28, 2014, http://www.ninds.nih.gov/disorders/brain_basics/know_your_brain.htm.

6. Arnsten, Mazure, and Sinha, "Everyday Stress."

7. Susan Weinschenk, PhD, "The True Cost of Multi-Tasking," *Psychology Today*, September 18, 2012, http://www.psychologytoday.com/blog/brain-wise/201209/the-true-cost-multi-tasking.

8. Jeremy Singer-Vine, "Open This Story in a New Tab," *Slate*, December 6, 2010, http://www.slate.com/articles/life/the_hive/2010/12/open_this_story_in_a_new_tab.html.

Chapter 9 Taming Our Perfectionist Instincts

1. Neil Fiore, PhD, *The Now Habit* (New York: Tarcher/Penguin, 2007), 24.

2. Kathi Lipp, "The Perfect Cup of Coffee," *Encouragement for Today*, September 17, 2014, http://proverbs31.org/devotions/devotion-author/kathi-lipp/#sthash.ekOHZY0i.dpuf.

3. Carol Dweck, *Mindset: The New Psychology of Success* (New York: Ballantine, 2007), 6.

4. Ibid., 7.

Chapter 10 Replacing Bad Habits with Good

1. Burka and Yuen, *Procrastination*, 90.

2. Charles Duhigg, *The Power of Habit* (New York: Random House, 2014), 14.

3. Ibid., 62.

4. Renee Swope, *A Confident Heart* (Grand Rapids: Revell, 2011), 221–23.

Chapter 11 Strengthening Willpower

1. "What You Need to Know about Willpower: The Psychological Science of Self-Control," American Psychological Association Help Center, accessed February 25, 2015, http://www.apa.org/helpcenter/willpower.aspx.

2. "Stanford Marshmallow Experiment," Wikipedia, accessed February 25, 2015, http://en.wikipedia.org/wiki/Stanford_marshmallow_experiment.

3. B. J. Casey et al., "Behavioral and Neural Correlates of Delay of Gratification 40 Years Later," *Proceedings of the National Academy of Sciences* 108, no. 36 (August 9, 2011): 14998–15003, doi:10.1073/pnas.1108561108.

4. Maria Konnikova, "The Struggles of a Psychologist Studying Self-Control," *The New Yorker*, October 9, 2014, http://www.newyorker.com/science/maria-konnikova/struggles-psychologist-studying-self-control.

5. Kathleen D. Vohs et al., "Making Choices Impairs Subsequent Self-Control: A Limited-Resource Account of Decision Making, Self-Regulation, and Active Initiative," *Journal of Personality and Social Psychology* (May 2008): 883–98.

6. Ibid., 897.

7. Tracy, *Eat That Frog!*, 3.

8. Tamara Lowe, *Get Motivated!* (New York: Doubleday, 2009), 27.

Chapter 12 Becoming a Wise Time Manager

1. Burka and Yuen, *Procrastination*, 194.

2. "Opportunity Cost," BusinessDictionary.com, accessed February 25, 2015, http://www.businessdictionary.com/definition/opportunity-cost.html.

3. Tracy, *Eat That Frog!*, 15.

4. Seth Godin, "The Jobs Only You Can Do," *Seth's Blog*, November 23, 2014, http://sethgodin.typepad.com/seths_blog/2014/11/index.html.

Chapter 13 Organizing Our Work

1. David Allen, *Getting Things Done* (New York: Penguin, 2001), 23.

2. Kathi Lipp and Cheri Gregory, *The Cure for the "Perfect" Life* (Eugene, OR: Harvest House, 2014), 99.

Chapter 14 Small Changes Matter

1. Erika Anderson, "21 Quotes from Henry Ford on Business, Leadership and Life," *Forbes*, May 31, 2013, http://www.forbes.com/sites/erikaandersen/2013/05/31/21-quotes-from-henry-ford-on-business-leadership-and-life/.

2. Nick Glass and Tim Hume, "The 'Hallelujah Moment' Behind the Invention of the Post-it Note," CNN, April 4, 2014, http://www.cnn.com/2013/04/04/tech/post-it-note-history/index.html.

Glynnis Whitwer, executive director of communications for Proverbs 31 Ministries, is a regular contributor to *Encouragement for Today*, the Proverbs 31 email devotional. She is the author of *Doing Busy Better*, *I Used to Be So Organized*, *When Your Child Hurts*, and *work@home*, and the coauthor of *Everyday Confetti*. She blogs regularly at www.glynniswhitwer.com.

glynnis whitwer

Room to Breathe

· · ·

GlynnisWhitwer.com

Proverbs 31
MINISTRIES

If you were inspired by *Taming Your To-Do List* and desire to deepen your own personal relationship with Jesus Christ, I encourage you to connect with Proverbs 31 Ministries.

Proverbs 31 Ministries exists to be a trusted friend who will take you by the hand and walk by your side, leading you one step closer to the heart of God through:

- ✳ Free online daily devotions
- ✳ Daily radio programs
- ✳ Books and resources
- ✳ Online Bible studies
- ✳ COMPEL writer's training:
  COMPELTRAINING.COM

To learn more about Proverbs 31 Ministries, call **877-731-4663** or visit **www.Proverbs31.org**.

Proverbs 31 Ministries
630 Team Rd., Suite 100
Matthews, NC 28105
Proverbs31.org

FIND FREEDOM IN THE

Gifts of Work and Rest

In this burden-lifting book, Glynnis Whitwer helps you examine your heart and your schedule in order to seek a healthy, holy, and enjoyable balance between work and rest. She shows you how to prioritize your goals and your time, how to be present in the moment as Jesus was, and how to find the freedom of true soul rest.

Revell
a division of Baker Publishing Group
www.RevellBooks.com

Available wherever books and ebooks are sold.